BRADFORD
IN 100 DATES

ALAN HALL

The History Press

For Amanda

First published 2015

The History Press
The Mill, Brimscombe Port
Stroud, Gloucestershire, GL5 2QG
www.thehistorypress.co.uk

© Alan Hall, 2015

The right of Alan Hall to be identified as the Author
of this work has been asserted in accordance with the
Copyright, Designs and Patents Act 1988.

British Library Cataloguing in Publication Data.
A catalogue record for this book is available from the British Library.

ISBN 978 0 7509 5853 0

Typesetting and origination by The History Press
Printed in Great Britain

Contents

Acknowledgements

Special thanks must go to Sue Caton and her staff at Bradford Local Studies Library, for helping me access much of the source material I have used. Thanks also to Matilda Richards of The History Press who suggested that I write this book. Last but not least, I want to thank my wife Amanda, who has once again been an encouragement to me in all kinds of ways.

Introduction

Let us be frank, apart from some interesting episodes in the early years of the English Civil War, Bradford has little noteworthy history prior to the opening of the Bradford Canal in 1774. This landmark event helped to catapult the town headlong into the Industrial Revolution, and within a generation or so Bradford had become an internationally known place to be reckoned with. Consequently, most of the events described in this book are from the nineteenth and twentieth centuries, with a few crucial ones from the twenty-first.

Taking the 100 dates as a whole, it soon becomes clear that, especially in the last 200 years, there must hardly have been a dull moment in Bradford. Its inhabitants have lived through wars, riots, fires, floods, strikes and social upheavals of a kind not necessarily found elsewhere. But as well as enduring all manner of trials and tribulation, there is clear evidence – certainly since the mid-nineteenth century – that the people of Bradford have developed a great pride in their city and in the achievements of its citizens. That pride continues right up to the present day.

The majority of the events and personalities featured in this book relate to Bradford as it existed before the local government boundary changes of 1974, but some references to places such as Bingley, Haworth, Saltaire and Keighley are also included because these communities, whether their inhabitants like it or not, are now part of Bradford. In many ways they always were. Haworth, for example, was part of the parish of Bradford from medieval times. Saltaire was the creation of a man who had made his fortune in Bradford and had been one of its first mayors before building his magnificent mill and model township on green and pleasant land just a few miles down the road from the dark Satanic mills in the centre of Bradford.

Researching and writing *Bradford in 100 Dates* has not only been a very enjoyable experience for me, it has also been something of an eye-opener. As a native of Bradford, I always assumed that I knew quite a bit about the city's history and heritage, but I had never heard of the deadly Bradford Sweet Poisoning of 1858 or the 1804 Festival of Bishop Blaise; nor did I know that people like Harry Houdini, Charlie Chaplin and Buffalo Bill's Wild West Show had all appeared here. I know now.

Bradford is a fascinating place, and I hope that this book will show that it has a fascinating history too.

Alan Hall, 2015

BRADFORD
IN 100 DATES

20 May

On this day, Bingley Market was granted its charter by King John. This makes it the oldest market with a royal charter in the Bradford Metropolitan District, although it is very likely that in Roman times there was a market in Ilkley, adjoining the fort that was built near the River Wharfe. Ilkley, known by the Romans as Olicana, was a military base with a garrison that had the task of keeping the local Celtic people, the Brigantes, in order and the roads across the Pennines secure.

The township of Bradford was granted a charter for a market by Henry III in 1251, and Keighley received its market charter in 1305, granted by Edward I.

Bingley's medieval butter cross and an eighteenth-century open-sided market hall have been rebuilt and are now located, along with the town's stocks, close to the refurbished market-place, which was opened in 2007. Bingley was a comparatively important place in the Middle Ages. It has been estimated that Bradford had a population of about 300 in 1379. Yet the poll tax returns for Bingley, just 6 miles from Bradford, show that in that same year there were 130 households, giving an estimated population of about 500, which was considerably larger than Bradford – or Leeds or Halifax for that matter. (J. James, *History of Bradford*)

9 September

On this day, King Charles I, perennially short of money, undertook the kind of asset-stripping that has become quite familiar to us in more recent times. He sold off the manor of Bradford for cash to four City of London financiers, and the right to collect the Bradford parish tithes was bought by one of his courtiers, John Maynard. This greatly angered Bradford's townspeople, especially the yeoman class who were increasingly keen to exercise their independence, for it all smacked of the worst kind of monarchical high-handedness.

There was also resentment over the Crown's attempts to increase the taxes on the export of cloth, especially as the collection of these taxes was frequently farmed out to corrupt favourites of the king. In short, the people of Bradford believed that Charles was misusing his royal position; he taxed them unfairly and carried out dubious practices that were detrimental to their commercial interests, whilst financially benefiting his London-based courtiers and favourites.

And, to cap it all, the king's wife was a Catholic. In fact many people believed that Charles was himself a Catholic in all but name. This was yet another reason why Bradford would remain firmly within the Parliamentarian fold during the forthcoming period of civil strife, for the town had developed a strong tradition of Puritanism and anti-Catholicism. The king was certainly not popular in Bradford. (J. James, *History of Bradford*; G. Firth, *A History of Bradford*)

18 December

During the English Civil War, the first Siege of Bradford was ended by the so-called Battle of the Steeple. This date saw the townspeople of Bradford, helped by reinforcements from Bingley and Halifax, successfully drive off the Royalist troops who were trying to capture the town. Bradford, staunchly Puritan and anti-Royalist, was firmly on the side of the Parliamentarians during the Civil War.

During the siege the parish church was used as a stronghold by the defenders, and wool packs were hung down the sides of the church tower to protect it against Royalist cannonballs. Much of the day's fighting took place around the parish church (now Bradford Cathedral) – hence the battle's name.

Because the townspeople, unlike their adversaries, were not professional soldiers, they were largely ignorant of the etiquette of warfare, so when a Royalist officer surrendered to a group of irregulars and asked for 'Quarter' he was hacked to death. This led to the term 'Bradford Quarter' being coined to describe those incidents throughout the war when people who had surrendered were nonetheless slaughtered out of hand. And when the Royalists returned to Bradford the following year, it was commonly supposed that they would be out for revenge and would show no mercy to the townspeople – they would be sure to exact 'Bradford Quarter'. (Bradford Library Service (ed.), *The Siege of Bradford*; A. Hall, *The Story of Bradford*)

30 June

At this time the Battle of Adwalton Moor was fought near Drighlington, a few miles from Bradford, between the Parliamentarians under Lord Fairfax and the Royalists under the Earl of Newcastle. Newcastle led an army of about 9,000 men; Fairfax had an army of about 4,000. Lord Fairfax's son, Sir Thomas, commanded the troops on the Parliamentarian's right flank and of crucial importance was the fact that the undulating terrain of the moor meant that he could not really see what was happening to the rest of the army to his left.

At first things went well for the Fairfaxes and Sir Thomas' musketeers inflicted heavy losses on the Royalist cavalry. However, things swung in the Royalists' favour after a charge by mounted pikemen broke through the Parliamentarian's left flank, causing the troops there to retreat. This was the key moment in the battle. Sir Thomas offered no support to his beleaguered comrades to his left for the simple reason that he was not aware that they were in difficulties. Seizing this advantage, the Royalists launched fresh cavalry charges and soon the entire Parliamentarian army was leaving the field and fleeing back towards Bradford. The Fairfaxes themselves fled to the safety of the Parliamentarian stronghold at Hull. During the battle, around 700 of their army were killed by the Royalists. (J. James, *History of Bradford*; B. Duckett and J. Waddington-Feather, *Bradford, History & Guide*; A. Hall, *The Story of Bradford*; Burne and Young, *The Battle of Adwalton Moor*; G. Firth, *A History of Bradford*)

2 July

On this day, the Earl of Newcastle's army surrounded Bradford after their victory at Adwalton Moor. The earl himself was ensconced at Bolling Hall, less than a mile from the town centre. Bradford was at his mercy and he intended to occupy the town the following day.

The inhabitants of the town feared the worst. Joseph Lister, who lived in Bradford, described in his journal the atmosphere in the town that Sunday night:

> Oh what a night and morning was that in which Bradford was taken! What weeping and wringing of hands! None expected to live any longer than till the enemies came into town, the Earl of Newcastle having charged his men to kill all …

To the surprise and immense relief of the townspeople, the massacre did not happen. A story soon began to circulate that Newcastle had had a change of heart whilst in bed at Bolling Hall on the Sunday night. It was said that a ghostly figure – a woman – appeared and begged him to 'Pity poor Bradford'. Whether or not he was really visited by a ghost (or even by a more tangible female) pleading Bradford's case, Newcastle certainly showed Bradford unexpected mercy. The remnants of the defeated Parliamentarian army surrendered to him the next day, but only a few people were actually killed when the Royalists moved in to occupy the town. (J. James, *History of Bradford*; B. Duckett and J. Waddington-Feather, *Bradford, History & Guide*; A. Hall, *The Story of Bradford*; Burne and Young, *The Battle of Adwalton Moor*; G. Firth, *A History of Bradford*)

18 March

This day saw Mary Sykes brought before the justice, Henry Tempest, at Bolling Hall and accused of witchcraft by several of her neighbours. This was Bradford's own participation in a spate of witch-hunting that was prevalent throughout England at this time.

Dorothy Rodes testified that Sykes had, by witchcraft, entered the bedroom of her young daughter, Sara, and seized her by the throat, after which the child suffered episodes of muscular spasms, palpitations and an inability to speak. Richard Booth testified that he had been cursed by Mary Sykes and, as a result, had lost many of his possessions. Henry Cordingley of Tong testified that Mary Sykes had cursed him several times since Christmas, since when several of his horses and cows had mysteriously died. Cordingley also claimed that on one occasion, going to check on his animals at midnight, he had encountered Mary Sykes sitting astride one of his cows; she then flew out of the cowshed window.

Tempest ordered Mary Sykes to be seized and physically examined by a team of six women. On her left side they discovered a strange wart, which was interpreted as being the third nipple with which witches were supposed to suckle the devil. As a result of this 'evidence', Mary Sykes was sent for trial at York Assizes. She was acquitted. (J. James, *History of Bradford*)

12 October

On this day a group of men from Bradford joined with others from Leeds and gathered at Farnley Wood, between Leeds and Morley. This was the so-called Farnley Wood Plot. The plotters, who had all been supporters of the Parliamentarians in the recent Civil War, intended to launch an uprising against Charles II and establish a republic. Now that the monarchy had been restored they feared, with some justification, that Puritan Dissenters, such as themselves, would be persecuted. They were also deeply suspicious of Charles' apparent sympathy towards Roman Catholics.

Henry Bradshaw of Manningham and John Lowcock, a saddler, were the ringleaders of the Bradford contingent. They had acquired a certain amount of weaponry and some horses, but the plot turned out to be rather a damp squib. Far fewer men turned up than was expected, so rather than setting off from Farnley Wood and seizing Leeds, as was planned, the plotters simply went back home.

That might have been the end of the matter, but one of the leaders of the Leeds contingent, Joshua Greathead, turned informer and gave the names of the plotters to the authorities. Twenty-six men were arrested, tried and subsequently executed for treason at York and Leeds. However, it seems that many of the Bradford contingent managed to evade arrest and it is likely that they fled abroad. (J. James, *History of Bradford*)

31 March

Edmund Robinson, a Haworth preacher, was executed at York on this day for coining and clipping. From his youth, Robinson had been involved in forging coins by using pewter instead of silver. Taking holy orders in the Church of England apparently did nothing to stop his nefarious activities, which also included clipping (shaving silver from coins), issuing forged marriage licences and conducting clandestine marriages. The York prison chaplain made the following somewhat understated comment before Robinson was hanged: 'His life, while a curate, was by no means suitable to his profession.'

In the late seventeenth and early eighteenth centuries, coining was a quite common occurrence in the remote western moors and hills of Bradford parish, and the authorities found it difficult to suppress. Robinson had, in fact, been tried on four earlier occasions for coining and clipping; he was acquitted twice and fined twice. The second fine was for the then astronomical sum of £500, but Robinson could presumably afford to pay this, as one of his criminal associates, Roger Preston, testified that in one half-year period Robinson had netted £1,300 from coining.

Presumably the authorities had had enough when Robinson was brought to trial for the fifth time – hence his execution. He had, rather understandably, already been dismissed from the Church of England. (J. James, *History of Bradford*)

16 May

This was the day that the Reverend William Grimshaw (1708–63) became curate at Haworth. Only Patrick Bronte, father of the famous sisters, is a better-known Haworth cleric.

Whilst Grimshaw's early life was characterised by a taste for gambling and drinking, by the time he came to Haworth he was a reformed character. He became renowned for his preaching, and his sermons became so popular that, in 1755, Haworth church had to be enlarged. He was a close friend and enthusiastic disciple of John Wesley, who frequently preached in Haworth. Like Wesley, Grimshaw never left the Church of England, but he was a leading figure in what became known as the Methodist Revival.

According to the nineteenth-century historian John James, Grimshaw 'exhibited more zeal than judgement'. He was not averse to using a horsewhip to put down 'the many rank vices' in Haworth. On one occasion he objected to horseracing on Haworth Moor, because it encouraged gambling. Unable to stop the race meeting in any other way, Grimshaw prayed fervently for rain. This duly came and it rained for three solid days, putting an end to the races. Such is the power of prayer!

In *Wuthering Heights*, Mr Lockwood has a nightmare in which he must endure the Reverend Jabes Branderham preaching an interminable sermon. Some commentators believe this to be Emily Bronte's satirical comment on Grimshaw's evangelical style. (J. James, *History of Bradford*)

18 July

On this day, Abraham Sharp, the mathematician and astronomer, died. He was born into a prosperous family that lived at Horton Hall in Little Horton, and although the precise date of his birth is unknown, he was baptised on 1 June 1653. After attending Bradford Grammar School he was apprenticed to a wool merchant, but he soon gave that up in order to study and teach mathematics. Sharp moved to London in the 1680s and worked at the Royal Observatory as the assistant and instrument maker to John Flamsteed, the first Astronomer Royal. His talent as a mathematician led to him being appointed Clerk of the King's Shipyard in Portsmouth.

On the death of his brother, his widowed sister-in law requested that he return to Horton Hall, the family home. This he did in 1694. He used some of his wealth to endow the first Presbyterian chapel in Bradford – the Sharps were Puritan Dissenters and Abraham's father had been financial secretary to Sir Thomas Fairfax during the Civil War. Back home in Bradford, Sharp continued his mathematical research, producing important work on logarithms.

A tablet commemorating his life stands in Bradford Cathedral. Translated from Latin it reads: 'He was rightly counted among the most accomplished mathematicians of his day. He enjoyed constant friendship with very famous men of the same repute, notably Flamsteed and the illustrious Newton.' (W. Cudworth, *Life and Correspondence of Abraham Sharp*; J. James, *History and Topography of Bradford*)

18 June

A mob pulled down the turnpike barriers at Bradford Moor and at Apperley Bridge on this day. An absence of adequate roads around Bradford had led to much frustration among the growing class of merchants. Improvements eventually came via the creation of turnpike trusts, private-sector initiatives whereby local businessmen and landowners obtained, through Act of Parliament, permission to charge tolls on a stretch of road. A proportion of the money thus gained was then reinvested in the maintenance and improvement of the highway. From a business point of view the turnpikes were a resounding success, for they improved communications considerably and so benefited trade. Bradford was first linked to the network of turnpikes in 1734, from which time it lay on a main road between Leeds and Manchester. Six years later, a second turnpike between Selby and Halifax was routed through Bradford.

However, many poorer people resented having to pay tolls to use the roads and this led to outbreaks of rioting and destruction. On 22 June 1753, the turnpike barriers at Tyersal and Wibsey Bankfoot were destroyed by a mob reported to be several hundred strong. Anti-turnpike rioting now spread quickly through the Bradford and Leeds area, and troops were summoned from York and Manchester to restore order. A crowd was fired on and there were several fatalities before the rioters were dispersed. (J. James, *History of Bradford*; B. Duckett and J. Waddington-Feather, *Bradford, History & Guide*; A. Hall, *The Story of Bradford*; G. Firth, *A History of Bradford*)

12 March

On this day the famous Bingley Five Rise Locks, a remarkable feat of engineering, opened for traffic. There are actually two flights of locks, Five Rise Locks and Three Rise Locks. (Technically these two flights are really staircases, with the top gate of one pound acting as the bottom gate of the pound above, and so on.) Five Rise Locks is the steepest flight of locks in the United Kingdom, with a rise of about 59 feet over a distance of 320 feet, giving a gradient of about one-in-five. The smaller Three Rise Locks, just a couple of hundred yards away, has a rise of about 30 feet. On the opening day a crowd estimated at 30,000 was in attendance to watch the first barge make the descent of Five Rise Locks.

In the same year that the Bingley locks were completed the Bradford Canal, 3 miles long with ten locks, was opened, linking the centre of Bradford to a waterway system which was to provide low-cost access to the burgeoning industrial regions of Yorkshire, Lancashire and beyond, including the ports of Hull and, eventually, Liverpool. This was a key event in Bradford's history. From now on the town's manufacturers had a facility that would enable them to trade coal, stone and iron with many parts of England and worsted cloth with the world at large. (J. James, *History of Bradford*; B. Duckett and J. Waddington-Feather, *Bradford, History & Guide*; A. Hall, *The Story of Bradford*; G. Firth, *A History of Bradford*; J. Fieldhouse, *Bradford*)

8 July

This day saw the *Leeds Intelligencer* report clear evidence of the way in which the canals were now starting to make a significant improvement to Bradford's woollen trade. A cargo of 200 sheets of raw wool was transported in two barges from Brigg in Lincolnshire to a Bradford warehouse, the journey taking only five days – six days earlier the fleeces had still been on the backs of the sheep!

The barges would have used the navigable River Ancholme from Brigg to the Humber Estuary, then the Aire and Calder Navigation – part river, part canal – to reach Leeds, from where the new canal to Shipley could be accessed. From Shipley the Bradford Canal would enable the barges to bring their goods right into the centre of the town; the terminal basin was below the parish church, close to where Canal Road enters Forster Square in modern times.

The *Leeds Mercury* reported that a week later (16 July 1777), a new service opened to convey goods between Leeds and Bradford using the canals. The service operated on three days a week. Three boats were used and the journey between the two towns took just a day. The Bradford-based proprietors of the service also arranged for carriages to convey goods by road on to Halifax from Bradford. (B. Duckett (ed.), *Bradford Chapters*)

19 December

On this day the *Leeds Mercury* reported that two gentlemen had been robbed of upwards of 40 guineas by a masked highwayman at the bottom of Horton Lane. As Bradford had no police force to speak of at this time, highwaymen and footpads usually got away with their crimes. In November 1754, the *Leeds Intelligencer* reported that Mr Shakelton and Mr Aked of Bradford were robbed by a highwayman on the road between Bradford and Halifax; the former losing 16*s* and a silver watch and the latter 13*s*.

The road to Halifax seems to have been particularly perilous. In March 1756, Richard Holmes and Abraham Wells, both of Bradford, were robbed on this road by two footpads armed with swords. Holmes was deprived of about 20*s* and Wells lost 3*s* 6*d*, though he was quick-thinking enough to save his watch and his gold by dropping them into the lining of his coat. And in December 1764, James Stables, a wealthy cloth merchant, had a lucky escape when he was accosted at Bradford Moor by a footpad who threatened to knock his brains out with a cudgel. Stables handed over all he had in one pocket, which was only 14½*d*. He then rode off with the bulk of his money intact, as it was in his other pocket. (B. Duckett (ed.), *Bradford Chapters*)

22 July

John Wesley, the founder of Methodism, preached in Baildon on this date. His sermon – on the text of St Mark's Gospel, chapter 3, verse 35 – was delivered from the window of a building, which is now an Indian restaurant.

Methodism quickly took a strong hold in Bradford, with a Wesleyan Society founded as early as 1747. Wesley visited Bradford on many occasions, the first time being in 1744, when he preached in Little Horton. He also preached at a hall in the centre of Bradford called the Cockpit, which was located near to where Centenary Square is today. This building was a hotbed of vice, gambling and drinking before being taken over by the Methodists in 1756. The Cockpit had the benefit of an open area to its front, which enabled people to stand outside and hear Wesley and other preachers even when the building was full. Wesley and his associates always drew large crowds wherever they preached.

Much of the appeal of Methodism to the people of Bradford was rooted in the town's long-standing tradition of Puritanism. Wesley himself always remained a member of the Church of England, but he favoured a simpler, more accessible form of worship, devoid of what he considered to be the excessive formality and ritual associated with the High Anglican Church. Bradford retains many Methodist chapels, some still in use, others not. (J. James, *History of Bradford*; B. Duckett and J. Waddington-Feather, *Bradford, History & Guide*; A. Hall, *The Story of Bradford*; G. Firth, *A History of Bradford*; J. Fieldhouse, *Bradford*)

20 April

On this day the Vestry made an order, forbidding people to allow 'pigs to run at large in the streets and highways of the township of Bradford'. The Vestry, which met in the vestry of the parish church, hence its name, was an unelected group of Bradford's leading inhabitants. At this time it was the only body with any kind of oversight of the town's affairs – not that anyone took much notice of the orders that it issued. In this particular case, for example, the Vestry minutes of May 1798 – three years later – noted that the problem of pigs running around in the streets was 'still continuing to be a very great nuisance'. The Vestry made another order: 'That Robert Wray, the beadle, with such assistance as he may procure, be appointed to carry out the order made as mentioned above into execution,' i.e. he was charged with making sure that people kept their pigs off the streets – or perhaps he was expected to round them up himself.

As late as 1825 this problem still persisted. The Board of Improvement Commissioners, which by then had superseded the Vestry, ordered: 'That Thomas Hoadley's pigs be not allowed to run loose and be fed in the Market Place.'

Clearly the townspeople of Bradford were rather reluctant to obey the voice of authority. Some things do not change. (J. James, *History of Bradford*)

1803

1 July

It was on this date that the Board of Improvement Commissioners, established by Act of Parliament, met for the first time at the Bulls Head Inn in Westgate. The commissioners, fifty-eight in number, were responsible for the following: '… paving, lighting, watching and improving the town of Bradford and part of the hamlet of Little Horton, and for removing and preventing all nuisances therein.'

The Board's activities were financed by rates levied on all townspeople occupying property of an annual value of at least £4. Only men with property worth £1,000 could become Commissioners, and nobody who made his living from selling alcohol was permitted to serve.

Unfortunately, the Board did not actually replace the Vestry, which still continued to meet, retaining the right to oversee such things as poor relief and the surveying of certain streets and thoroughfares. So from the start there was confusion over where power lay and who was responsible for what. In addition, the Commissioners had no jurisdiction over nearby Bowling, Manningham and the bulk of Horton, all of which were about to experience the same kind of chaotic expansion as Bradford. These three localities, which had a combined population of over 30,000 by the 1840s, lacked any kind of local government until they became part of the incorporated borough of Bradford in 1847. (J. James, *History of Bradford*; W. Cudworth, *Historical Notes on the Bradford Corporation*)

1803

20 September

Titus Salt was born on this day. He became not just one of the most successful of Bradford's textile manufacturers, but also one of the great philanthropists of the Victorian age, especially with the building of Saltaire – a model township designed to provide his workers with a much healthier environment than was the norm elsewhere. In 1853, to celebrate his fiftieth birthday and the grand opening of Salts Mill, he laid on a banquet for 3,500 of his workers. This took place in the mill's combing shed and was reckoned at the time to be perhaps the largest dinner party ever set down at one time. Salt was Mayor of Bradford in 1848 and, despite a trade recession during his term of office, he saw fit to offer work to 100 unemployed wool combers, as much out of a spirit of Christian compassion as a desire to make any money.

Salts Mill ceased textile production in 1986 and for a time it was threatened with demolition. Fortunately it was rescued by a Bradford-born entrepreneur called Jonathan Silver, and by the twenty-first century the mill had been transformed. Nowadays it houses an art gallery, an IT company and a range of upmarket shops. Saltaire itself is now a UNESCO World Heritage Site, a fitting memorial to Titus Salt.

Salt died in 1876. (J. Reynolds, *Saltaire*; R. Suddards, *Titus of Salt*)

3 February

On this day the Festival of Bishop Blaise (sometimes spelt Blaize) was celebrated by a huge procession of masters, apprentices, spinners, wool combers and the like, which wound its way through Bradford and the outlying communities, before ending at the Bull's Head Inn in Westgate, where a sumptuous feast was consumed by the town's great and good.

Blaise was an early Christian bishop in Armenia. According to legend he was martyred by being hacked to death with iron wool combs. He was therefore an appropriate choice to be the patron saint of wool combers and, by association, the patron saint of all textile workers, as well as the patron saint of Bradford itself. A statue of Blaise, wool comb in hand, adorns the front of the Wool Exchange in the centre of Bradford.

Bradford's Blaise Festival only took place every seven years. Although the first mention of it is in 1769, it may have its origins in the Middle Ages. The 1804 festival was noted for its size and grandeur, which to observers at the time seemed to reflect Bradford as a place to be reckoned with. The festivals of 1811 and 1818 were equally elaborate affairs, but the 1825 festival had a mixed reception, as the wool combers were in a bitter dispute with the mill owners in that year. (J. James, *History of Bradford*)

1 January

Samuel Cunliffe Lister (d. 1906) was born on this date. Originally intending to train as a Church of England vicar, Lister decided instead to follow his father into the textile trade. He became one of the great textile barons of Victorian Bradford and his gigantic Manningham Mills, completed in 1873, still dominates the skyline to the north-west of the city. In more recent times it has been refurbished as Lister Mill, a series of apartments.

As well as being one of the most successful businessmen of the time, Lister was also an inventor. His development of an effective wool-combing machine in the 1840s revolutionised Bradford's textile industry and led to the town becoming the centre of the British worsted trade. The invention made Lister extremely rich, but later he almost bankrupted himself by trying to perfect techniques to produce velvet from silk waste. Eventually his attempts were successful and he became a multi-millionaire. Velvet was produced at Manningham Mills up to the end of the twentieth century and it was exported all over the world.

Lister Park, formerly the grounds of Lister's home, is now Bradford's premier park. Towards the end of his life Lister donated money for the establishment of Cartwright Hall, which stands within the park. Opened by Lister (by then Lord Masham) in 1904, it is the city's principal art gallery. (J. James, *History of Bradford*; B. Duckett and J. Waddington-Feather, *Bradford, History & Guide*; A. Hall, *The Story of Bradford*; G. Firth, *A History of Bradford*; J. Fieldhouse, *Bradford*)

30 July

On this day, Emily Brontë, the author of *Wuthering Heights*, was born in Thornton where her father, Patrick, was the curate. In the early 1820s the family moved to Haworth. Career opportunities for women of Emily's class were virtually non-existent at that time; teaching or working as a governess were really the only options. Unlike her sisters, Emily never worked as a governess and only worked as a teacher for a few months. The rest of her life was spent in Haworth, undertaking household duties, walking on the nearby moors – and secretly writing.

As children the Brontë sisters and their brother Branwell wrote stories and poems about two imaginary countries called Angria and Gondal. This was an understandable form of escapism, given that their mother was dead, their father was rather austere and their lives were circumscribed by Haworth, which was a rough and ready industrial boom town, surrounded by inhospitable countryside.

Emily probably started to write *Wuthering Heights* in 1845. Published in 1847, it was her only novel, although she may have been working on another when she died the following year.

Wuthering Heights met with mixed reviews when it was first published, principally because many reviewers found it shocking and unclassifiable. Nowadays it is generally recognised as a work of genius. (A. Hall, *The Story of Bradford*)

1825

8 June

A serious strike commenced in Bradford on 8 June 1825 and lasted twenty-three weeks. The handloom weavers and hand wool combers had organised themselves into the Combers and Weavers Union, and they set about pressing the worsted manufacturers for union recognition and improvements in pay. The manufacturers responded by attempting to coerce the workers into signing a petition renouncing the union and the children of those who refused to sign were dismissed from the spinning mills where they worked. This meant losing an important part of a family's income. The union therefore felt compelled to call a strike. People throughout Britain soon became aware of the dispute and £20,000 was raised to support the strikers, but ultimately the action failed.

The strike was really about the future of the worsted industry, how it would function and develop in an increasingly mechanised environment and, in particular, where the locus of power would lie in this new industrialised world. After the failure of the strike, the manufacturers were able to develop the worsted trade in ways that suited them best and the workers were forced to comply, or starve. Soon to become an anachronism, the handloom weavers and hand wool combers were still employable for a time, but only as a pool of out-workers for use when required by the employers to complement the mill-based operatives. (D.G. Wright, *The Chartist Risings in Bradford*; J. James, *History of Bradford*; B. Duckett and J. Waddington-Feather, *Bradford, History & Guide*; A. Hall, *The Story of Bradford*; G. Firth, *A History of Bradford*)

16 October

Richard Oastler (1789–1861) published his famous letter in the *Leeds Mercury* concerning the plight of children working in Bradford mills on this day:

> The very streets which receive the droppings of an Anti-Slavery Society are every morning wet by the tears of innocent victims at the accursed shrine of avarice, who are compelled not by the cart whip of the negro slave driver, but by the dread of the equally appalling thong or strap of the overlooker to hasten, half-dressed but not half-fed, to those magazines of British infantile slavery, the worsted mills in the town and neighbourhood of Bradford. Thousands of little children, both male and female, but principally female, from seven to fourteen years of age, are daily compelled to labour from six in the morning to seven in the evening … with only thirty minutes allowed for eating and recreation.

Oastler's letter was the start of a campaign that eventually led to the Factory Act of 1847. This limited the hours that women and young children could be employed, although it was not until 1861 that the provisions of the Act were extended to all workplaces.

A bronze statue of Oastler stands in Northgate, Bradford, depicting him with two small factory children. It was unveiled in 1869 by the Earl of Shaftesbury, the century's foremost advocate of better working conditions for children. (B. Duckett and J. Waddington-Feather, *Bradford, History & Guide*; A. Hall, *The Story of Bradford*; G. Firth, *A History of Bradford*)

20 November

On this day there was a riot in the middle of Bradford when the Guardians of the Poor met at the Court House to put into operation the Poor Law Amendment Act of 1834, which required parishes to group together to set up workhouses. These were to be made deliberately harsh, as it was thought this would compel people to seek work rather than poor relief.

Unfortunately, the Poor Law Commission, which formulated the Act, had neglected to consider conditions in the newly industrialised areas of the North of England, where workers were more susceptible to temporary periods of unemployment caused by trade fluctuations. The fear was that at such times entry into the dreaded workhouse would be inevitable. There was a trade slump in Bradford in 1837, so it was not surprising that people took to the streets. Bradford's Court House was attacked by a crowd estimated to have been at least 5,000 strong. After the Riot Act was read a company of the 15th Hussars was dispatched from Leeds to deal with the mob, which was reluctant to disperse, even when fired on. It was only when it started to rain heavily at about ten o' clock in the evening that the rioters began to go home.

Only five rioters were brought to trial and four served surprisingly lenient prison sentences of one month for rioting. (A. Hall, *The Story of Bradford*; G. Firth, *A History of Bradford*; J. James, *History of Bradford*)

2 June

On this day the Chartists, who were agitating for Parliamentary reform, tried to launch an uprising in Bradford and throughout the West Riding. In an attempt to remedy their increasingly desperate situation, the handloom weavers and hand wool combers – believing that their livelihood was being destroyed by machines – had gathered under the umbrella of Chartism.

Chartism was essentially a political movement that sought to reform Parliament as a first step towards alleviating Britain's economic problems and bringing about social justice. The Chartists demanded such things as universal male suffrage, payment for MPs and secret ballots. Bradford's handloom weavers and hand wool combers were not necessarily interested in these parliamentary reforms – they simply wanted a return to a pre-industrial society where they would have plenty of work and a certain amount of independence, rather than being forced into becoming slaves to the mill-owners and their new steam-powered machines.

The uprising came to nothing, but more outbreaks of Chartist violence were to come. Two years later, Thomas Drake, a handloom weaver from Thornton, led a series of attacks known as the Plug Plot Riots, against a number of Bradford mills. Drake's followers sabotaged several boilers and mill dams to prevent the power looms from running, but repairs were soon made and the mills continued to function. (D.G. Wright, *The Chartist Risings in Bradford*)

1 July

At the height of 'Railway Mania', which was sweeping the country, the railway came to Bradford. A line was opened that ran from a station at the end of Market Street (later to become Forster Square Station) to Wellington Station in Leeds. Although not the most direct route, it was the one which provided the fewest engineering problems, as it followed the route of the Bradford Canal to Shipley and the Leeds and Liverpool Canal from Shipley to Leeds along comparatively level terrain. The coming of the railway heralded the eventual demise of the Bradford Canal.

Eight years later, on 1 August 1854, a second railway line was opened. This one followed a shorter route between Bradford and Leeds via Pudsey. Bradford was now firmly on the railway map, but the town lacked a through-route that would, as the railway network expanded, have linked destinations to the north of Bradford with those to the south. From the early twentieth century to the present day, various schemes to create such a through-route have been mooted, but nothing has been built. Consequently, Bradford, in terms of railway provision (if nothing else), has had to play second fiddle to Leeds.

Nevertheless, Bradford achieved some railway fame on 1 June 1874, when the very first Pullman train in Britain made its maiden journey from Bradford to St Pancras. (A. Whitaker and B. Myland, *Railway Memories No. 4: Bradford*)

9 June

Bradford received its charter of incorporation on this date. Throughout the first half of the nineteenth century, Bradford had been rather like a town in the American wild west, with very little in the way of governance or law and order. Now the town was an incorporated borough and some order could be imposed. The township of Bradford itself was duly divided into four wards, designated North, South, East and West. Manningham, Great Horton, Little Horton and Bowling also became wards of the new borough. There were to be fourteen aldermen and forty-two councillors, each of whom had to own property of at least £1,000 to qualify, and the franchise was to consist of all males who were householders.

There was also to be a mayor. Bradford's first mayor was Robert Milligan, a Scot who had settled in Bradford in 1810 and had subsequently become a leading stuff (worsted cloth) merchant. Like many who were to follow him in the early days of the mayoralty, Milligan was a staunch Liberal.

Soon there was a police force and also a somewhat cleaner water supply. Bradford's first public park was opened shortly afterwards, named after Sir Robert Peel. And beneath the town's brand new coat of arms was the motto *Labor Omnia Vincit* ('Work Conquers All'). After half a century of unregulated growth and near-chaos, things were perhaps beginning to improve. (J. James, *History of Bradford*; W. Cudworth, *Historical Notes on the Bradford Corporation*; B. Duckett and J. Waddington-Feather, *Bradford, History & Guide*; A. Hall, *The Story of Bradford*; G. Firth, *A History of Bradford*)

29 May

A pitched battle was fought in Bradford between the Chartists and the forces of law and order on this day. The year 1848 marked the zenith of the Chartist movement in England, and it was also a year of revolution throughout Europe. In Bradford, a hotbed of unrest, the Chartists had armed themselves with pikes and openly drilled in the town for several weeks.

The police mounted an operation to arrest the local Chartist ringleader, a man called Jefferson. However, they were confronted by a large mob in Adelaide Street, off Manchester Road, and a furious conflict took place. The police were armed with cutlasses and the special constables had staves, but they were unable to prevail against the mob, which attacked them with stones and bludgeons. The Chartists were only dispersed by a squadron of fully armed dragoons after the police and special constables had suffered an ignominious defeat and been forced to retreat. Many people were wounded.

After 1848, Chartism declined rapidly and Bradford's handloom weavers and hand wool combers, who had been the main supporters of Chartism in Bradford, were forced to give up every vestige of their traditional independence and seek employment in the mills. By 1850 the worst of the economic depression was over and Bradford began a period of expansion and growing prosperity that lasted for a generation. (D.G. Wright, *The Chartist Risings in Bradford*)

13 August

On this day a public meeting was held to decide how best to commemorate Sir Robert Peel, the champion of free trade, who had died earlier that year. Bradford's civic leaders and industrialists viewed the principle of free trade as something akin to an article of religious faith, so Peel was much revered.

It was decided to create a public park – Peel Park – in the great man's honour, and this duly opened in 1853 in the Undercliffe area of the town. It was Bradford's first public park, 56 acres in size. Public subscription paid for the land, which was then handed over to the Corporation in 1870.

On 6 November 1855, a large bronze statue of Peel was unveiled in Peel Square, in those days near the bottom of Leeds Road. A crowd of 30,000 was said to have attended the unveiling. The statue was moved to its present location in Peel Park in 1926.

Since 1998 the annual Bradford Mela has been held in Peel Park. This is a two-day celebration of mainly South Asian culture – dance, music, displays and fairground attractions. When it was first held in Bradford in 1988 it was the first such event to be held in the UK, or indeed Europe, and it continues to be the largest mela in Europe, with upwards of 100,000 visitors in recent years. (W. Cudworth, *Round About Bradford*; J. James, *History of Bradford*)

1853

29 August

St George's Hall was opened on this day. Paid for by public subscription, it was designed by the Bradford architects Lockwood and Mawson, and was really Bradford's first public building, constructed just at the time when a certain amount of civic pride was beginning to develop in the town. The town council met here for some of its monthly meetings until the Town Hall was built in the 1870s. In 1854, Dickens read extracts from his new book *Bleak House* in the hall, for which he received the then princely sum of £100; he praised the hall's excellent acoustics (there were no microphones in those days), which many speakers and musicians since that time have also noted.

The hall was also used for political meetings, notably during the Manningham Mills strike of 1890–91, when it became the venue for several rallies of support for the strikers. Churchill was attacked by suffragettes at a political meeting in 1910 and supposedly had to seek refuge under the stage.

Over the course of its long history, St George's Hall has hosted events as diverse as all-in wrestling bouts, exhibitions of escapology by Harry Houdini, film shows and regular appearances by comedians such as Ken Dodd, but it is as a concert hall that it is best known. It may be the oldest concert hall in Britain still in use. (G. Sheeran, *The Buildings of Bradford*; P. Leach and N. Pevsner, *The Buildings of England: Yorkshire West Riding*)

1854

1 August

Undercliffe Cemetery was consecrated by the Bishop of Ripon on this date. The cemetery was urgently needed because of the rapid increase in Bradford's population in the previous half-century. Churchyards could no longer cope with the demand for burial plots, so the Bradford Cemetery Company was set up in 1849 to tackle the problem. Undercliffe Cemetery quickly became well known for its grandiose sepulchres and mausoleums, built to house the remains of Bradford's wealthy and prominent citizens. For this reason it is possibly second only to Highgate Cemetery in London as a fine example of a Victorian cemetery.

The cemetery was initially divided into two sections – the western side for Anglican burials and the eastern side for Nonconformists, who comprised a substantial number of Bradford's eminent families throughout the nineteenth century.

The cemetery now has Grade 2 status as a place of special historic interest. In 1977 the administration of the cemetery was taken over by the Undercliffe Cemetery Charity, though the site continues to be owned by Bradford Council.

Because of its impressive appearance, the cemetery has been a location for several feature films, notably *Billy Liar* (1963). Billy, played by Tom Courtenay, attempts to seduce his girlfriend Barbara (played by Helen Fraser) in the cemetery, but much to his frustration she is only interested in eating an orange. (C. Clark and R. Davison, *In Loving Memory: The Story of Undercliffe Cemetery*)

10 September

On this day, news of the fall of Sebastopol in the Crimea reached Bradford. This stimulated a week-long celebration; the bells of the parish church were rung, flags were displayed and bonfires lit. Many of the town's public buildings and warehouses were adorned with illuminated decorations.

At the end of the week a grand fete was held in Peel Park; bands played, there was a firework display, cannons were fired and an ox was roasted. Some time after the Crimean War, two captured Russian cannon were presented to the Peel Park Committee to be displayed in the park, but these have since been lost.

One aspect of this huge outburst of patriotic fervour was a significant amount of public drunkenness. Wisely perhaps, the police tended to turn a blind eye to this, possibly recalling how difficult it had been in the recent past to impose law and order on the rowdier elements of Bradford's populace.

Drunkenness was a perennial problem. In 1850 there were more than 150 beershops in Bradford. A report commissioned by Titus Salt at the time stated that 'scarcely any of them can be described as decent and orderly houses of entertainment … some are in fact brothels under another name'. The passing of the 1868 Beer Bill gave the Corporation the power to close ninety of the worst-conducted public houses. (J. James, *History of Bradford*; A. Hall, *The Story of Bradford*)

1855

31 October

On this day, Joseph Wright (d. 1930) was born in Thackley to poor parents, and at the age of 6 he was working in a local quarry. Later he worked at Salts Mill. Barely literate, even at the age of 15, Wright taught himself to read by studying the Bible and Bunyan's *Pilgrim's Progress*.

He became fascinated by language and, now that he had gained some mastery of written English, he set about learning French, German and Latin. In 1876 he went to study at the prestigious University of Heidelberg in Germany, walking from Antwerp to Heidelberg to save money. On his return to England he enrolled at the Yorkshire College of Science (now Leeds University), supporting himself by teaching, and in 1885 he returned to Heidelberg to complete a Ph.D.

He came back to England in 1888. At that time Max Muller was Professor of Philology at Oxford University and the most eminent philologist in Europe. He appointed Wright as his deputy.

In 1901, Wright himself became Professor of Philology at Oxford, and he held the post until he retired in 1925. He specialised in Germanic languages but was also deeply interested in English dialects. Between 1895 and 1905, Wright, assisted by his wife, Elizabeth, produced his *English Dialect Dictionary* in six volumes – even today it is regarded as the definitive work on English dialects. (A. Hall, *The Story of Bradford*)

18 October

On this day there occurred an incident that became known as the Bradford Sweet Poisoning. William Hardaker, known as 'Humbug Billy', sold sweets from a market stall in what was later to become Kirkgate Market. As was the usual custom in the trade, Hardaker's sweets were bulked out by adding plaster of Paris or powdered limestone, colloquially known as 'daft'. This reduced the manufacturing costs significantly, as sugar was an expensive item.

On this particular occasion, a Shipley pharmacist had mistakenly supplied Hardaker's associate, James Appleton, with arsenic trioxide instead of plaster of Paris. Appleton made a batch of humbugs that day using 40 pounds of sugar, 4 pounds of peppermint gum and 12 pounds of arsenic trioxide.

That evening, Hardaker sold 5 pounds of the poisonous sweets at 3 halfpence for 2 ounces. Within a day or so, 200 people – mainly children – had become seriously ill and twenty had died. At first it was thought that the deaths were a result of cholera, but the true cause was soon established and those involved were brought to trial. However, the charges were subsequently dropped and the deaths were deemed to have been the result of a tragic accident. There was a public outcry, eventually leading to the Pharmacy Act of 1868, which imposed tighter controls on pharmacies. Measures were also taken to regulate the adulteration of foodstuffs. (G. Sheeran, *The Bradford Poisoning of 1858*)

1859

6 June

This day saw the whole of the centre of Bradford experience a quite devastating flood, caused by four hours of torrential rain. The nineteenth-century historian John James described the storm as:

> ... the most dreadful ever witnessed here. Rain fell in torrents, intermixed with large hailstones. The streets were rapidly inundated, as the beck, owing to its contraction by injudicious building on its sides, and over it, overflowed. The lower parts of the town were completely flooded, perhaps to an extent never before known.

It was estimated that the cost of the damage caused by the flood amounted to more than £30,000.

The description of the storm and the subsequent flood bears an uncanny resemblance to two similar occurrences a century later. On 20 September 1946, the city centre was again flooded after 2 inches of rain fell in two hours. £1 million of damage was done. And on 1 July 1968, an extremely violent storm left the centre of Bradford under water once more. Around 1 inch of water fell in fifteen minutes. Of particular concern was the flooding of several recently constructed pedestrian subways. For a time it was feared that people might have drowned in them; frogmen were deployed to recover any bodies. Fortunately there were no deaths, but damage in excess of £2 million was caused. (J. James, *History of Bradford*; A. Hall, *The Story of Bradford*)

20 July

Margaret McMillan was born on this date. A Christian socialist, she came to Bradford in 1893 at the invitation of the Independent Labour Party and became a key figure on the Bradford School Board. Horrified by the conditions in which many of the children of Bradford's poor were living, she was instrumental in promoting a range of far-reaching reforms, notably a school meals service, a school medical inspection service, school baths, better facilities for handicapped children and the beginnings of a free nursery education system – all of which were successfully pioneered in Bradford during her time in the city or shortly after she left.

She was present at the very first medical inspection of children, held at Usher Street Elementary School in 1899, at which it was discovered that more than 100 of the pupils inspected had not removed their clothes for between six and eight months. This led her to press Bradford Corporation to introduce measures to educate parents about basic hygiene. Her own health suffered because of overwork and she left Bradford in 1902 to live in the South of England. When her health improved she continued her pioneering work, notably in Deptford.

Margaret McMillan died in 1931. A Bradford primary school is named after her, as is the McMillan School of Teaching, Health and Care at Bradford College. (M. McMillan, *The Life of Rachel McMillan*; B. Parker (ed.), *Education in Bradford 1870–1970*; A. Hall, *The Story of Bradford*)

29 January

On this day, Frederick Delius was born in Bradford. Educated at Bradford Grammar School, he was expected to join the family firm of wool merchants, a career for which he had neither interest nor aptitude. After an unsuccessful period managing a Florida orange plantation, Delius enrolled at the Leipzig Conservatoire in 1886. Later he lived for a time in Paris, where he met the playwright August Strindberg and the artists Paul Gauguin and Edvard Munch.

By the early twentieth century, Delius had become famous and today he is recognised as a major English composer whose work is often still performed.

For much of his life, Delius lived in Grez-sur-Loing in France, where he died in 1934, blind and paralysed from the effects of the tertiary stage of syphilis. He was made a freeman of Bradford in 1932. The honour was bestowed on him in Grez by a party of Bradford's civic dignitaries who travelled to France for the occasion.

Delius is buried in the village of Limpsfield, Surrey. Despite a reluctance to return to his birthplace, he apparently never lost his Yorkshire accent, and even though most of his life was spent in France, he retained a strong interest in cricket, a game that he had played with enthusiasm as a young man in Bradford. (B. Duckett (ed.), *The German Immigrants: Their Influence in 19th Century Bradford*)

9 August

Lord Palmerston, the prime minister at the time, laid the foundation stone of the Wool Exchange, designed by Lockwood and Mawson. By now the Corporation and Bradford's leading businessmen (usually, of course, the same people) were so imbued with municipal self-confidence that they organised a celebratory event which was verging on the outrageous in its pomp and circumstance. Church bells were rung, flags were flown, and there was a nineteen-gun salute in Peel Park. Approximately 100 carriages, attended by two military bands, drove in procession from Peel Park to the site of the Exchange on Market Street. In the evening, Palmerston was the guest of the Corporation at a grand dinner held in St George's Hall, where the Bradford Choral Society greeted him with a rendition of 'See the Conquering Hero Comes'. The only fly in the ointment, apparently, was a demonstration by a large number of working men in the streets of the town who steadfastly refused to cheer the distinguished visitor. Their silent protest was because of Palmerston's stubborn refusal to countenance an extension of the franchise.

The Wool Exchange was the hub of Bradford's textile trade until the 1960s, by which time the city's world-renowned position as 'Worstedopolis' had all but ended. Nowadays the Wool Exchange building provides an excellent location for a Waterstones bookshop. (W. Cudworth, *Historical Notes on the Bradford Corporation*)

16 July

On this day, Bradford's first daily newspaper, *The Bradford Daily Telegraph*, was launched. At the time, political power in Bradford was firmly in the hands of the Liberal Party and was to remain so until the later years of the nineteenth century, so it is not surprising that *The Bradford Daily Telegraph* had a Liberal editorial slant. There had been earlier newspapers in Bradford, notably *The Bradford Observer*, founded in 1834. Again, this was a Liberal newspaper, but for many years it was a weekly rather than a daily publication. At 7*d* a copy it was also much more expensive than *The Bradford Daily Telegraph*, which cost a mere halfpenny per copy. Probably the first Bradford-based newspaper was *The Bradford Courier*, which first appeared in 1825, but it ceased publication in 1828.

When the fortunes of the Conservative Party improved in Bradford in the 1890s, a new newspaper, *The Bradford Daily Argus*, was launched with an editorial bias towards the Conservatives. Despite a possible difference of political stance, *The Bradford Daily Argus* merged with *The Bradford Daily Telegraph* in 1926, and the resulting *Bradford Telegraph and Argus* had its first edition on 15 December that year. In 1947 the word 'Bradford' was dropped and the newspaper became simply *The Telegraph and Argus*, which it remains to this day. (W. Cudworth, *Worstedopolis*)

17 February

On this day, William Edward Forster (1818–86), the Liberal MP for Bradford, presented his Elementary Education Bill to Parliament, thus laying the foundations of compulsory education in England. The proposed legislation was not without controversy, particularly regarding the provision of religious education in schools. And some critics felt that the plan to establish school boards in areas where there was inadequate voluntary school provision would be a needless additional cost for ratepayers.

The rationale behind compulsory schooling was never purely educational. By 1870 legislation had forbidden the employment of very young children in factories. This meant that whilst the adults in a family might still be working long hours, their children could well be totally unsupervised and therefore at risk. There were reports of gangs of children wandering the streets of towns and cities, breaking the law and generally causing annoyance. Confining children every day in schools, where they would not be a nuisance to the public, and where they could be instructed in the rudiments of civilised behaviour (and some basic literacy) was therefore an appealing notion for many.

Forster was recognised as an important reformer and philanthropist. A major square in Bradford was named after him, and some years later the railway station adjoining the square also took his name. Only two Victorians had railway termini named after them: Forster and Queen Victoria. (B. Parker (ed.), *Education in Bradford 1870–1970*)

9 September

Bradford's Town Hall (now usually called City Hall) was formally opened on this date. Lockwood and Mawson's design of the magnificent main structure was supposedly influenced by Amiens Cathedral, although the clock tower is a copy of the campanile of the Palazzo Vecchio in Florence. Around the façade of the building are statues of English monarchs and – unusually – one of Oliver Cromwell. Bradford was a staunch supporter of the Parliamentarian cause during the English Civil War, and a tradition of dissent continued into the nineteenth century when the Town Hall was built.

When the statue of Cromwell was due to be hauled into place, the gang of Irish labourers charged with the task was rumoured to be planning to drop it 'accidentally on purpose' so that it would be smashed to pieces. Cromwell was traditionally loathed in Ireland because of the atrocities – such as the massacre at Drogheda – perpetrated by his soldiers. The rumour came to the attention of Bradford Corporation and the Irishmen were given a day's holiday. A gang of English labourers, who presumably bore no malice towards Cromwell, was quickly hired to carry out the task instead and Cromwell was safely hauled into his place on the façade of City Hall, where he remains to this day. (G. Sheeran, *The Buildings of Bradford*; P. Leach and N. Pevsner, *The Buildings of England: Yorkshire West Riding*)

29 March

This was the day that Bradford Reform Synagogue in Bowland Street, Manningham, was consecrated. The synagogue was built in a Moorish or Islamic revival style, featuring bands of brown and red sandstone. It is possibly the oldest reform synagogue in the country outside London. Joseph Strauss (1845–1922), one of the first reform rabbis in England, came to Bradford in 1873 to become the founding rabbi of the synagogue.

A community of German wool merchants, most of whom were Jewish, settled in Bradford from the 1840s onwards, attracted by the commercial opportunities which the rapidly expanding town offered. The magnificent warehouses, built in the area now known as Little Germany, bear witness to this community's success. Some of its members also became civic leaders of Bradford; for example Jacob Moser was lord mayor in 1910–11. Moser was a prominent philanthropist who gave thousands of pounds to charitable causes.

Bradford's Jewish community declined in numbers during the twentieth century, and by the twenty-first century the synagogue, in urgent need of repairs, was in danger of closing (the city's Orthodox Synagogue in nearby Spring Gardens, founded in 1906, had already closed in 1970). However, in 2013 Manningham's Muslim community came to the rescue, raising money to save the building in the interests of multi-faith friendship, thus preserving an important place of worship and a significant part of Bradford's history. (C.C. Aronsfield, *German Jews in 19th Century Bradford*)

2 February

Bradford's first tram service began to operate on this day. The route was from Rawson Square to the gates of Lister Park via Manningham Lane, a comparatively level journey for the horse-drawn trams to tackle. On 8 August that same year, a second route was opened from the town centre to Stanningley via Leeds Road. The trams on this route were steam-powered because of the steep gradients to be climbed.

At this time the trams were operated by private companies, but in 1898 Bradford Corporation opened its own tram routes from the town centre, one to Bolton Junction and another to Great Horton.

In 1902 the Corporation bought out the private operators and the following year the system became fully electrified. New routes were opened right up to the outbreak of the First World War, the last piece in the tramway jigsaw being the service from Bingley post office to Crossflatts.

In the inter-war years, Bradford's trams were increasingly superseded by trolley buses and motor buses. Trolley buses were more efficient on Bradford's hilly routes and motor buses were obviously more flexible than trams. On 6 May 1950 the last Bradford tram made its final journey from the city centre to Odsal Top. Trams came back into fashion in the late twentieth century, notably in Manchester and Sheffield, but not as yet in Bradford. (D.M. Coates, *Bradford City Tramways*)

1882

23 June

On this day the Bradford Technical School was formally opened by the Prince of Wales. The school had its origins as the Bradford Mechanics Institute, which was founded in 1832 by a group of manufacturers and philanthropists. They wanted to provide some general education for working people, as well as providing courses that would serve Bradford's industries. Fifty years later, vocational courses geared to the needs of the textile industries were seen as paramount, as there was a real fear that Bradford might be losing its pre-eminent position in the wool trade to foreign competitors.

Before long the school was renamed Bradford Technical College. It was taken over by Bradford Corporation in 1899, mainly because local businessmen were not prepared to provide the college with sufficient financial backing. In 1904 the School of Art was founded as an offshoot of the college.

From the early twentieth century, various attempts were made to achieve university status for the college, but with no success. However, in 1959, Bradford Institute of Technology was founded to provide degree-level higher education, whilst Bradford Technical College continued to provide non-degree courses. In 1966 the institute finally became the University of Bradford, with Harold Wilson as its first chancellor.

Nowadays the university's Peace Studies Department has a particularly high reputation, as does the School of Management. (W. Cudworth, *Worstedopolis*)

28 December

On this day fifty-four people were killed and more than fifty seriously injured when the chimney of Newlands Mill collapsed and fell onto the mill building. Newlands Mill was part of a giant complex of mills between Parma Street and Upper Castle Street in West Bowling. About 2,000 people worked there, including many children. Indeed the youngest victim of the disaster, Susan Woodhead, was aged 8, and more than half of those killed were aged 15 or younger. Forty of the fifty-four victims were women and girls. There would have been more deaths, but many employees had gone home for their breakfasts when the chimney collapsed.

The chimney was 255 feet high and weighed 4,000 tons. It was already showing signs of stress as early as 1866, the reason being that it had been built over a warren of primitive mine shafts and old tunnels; coal and iron had been mined in this part of West Bowling for centuries.

By 1882 the state of the chimney was causing real concern – cracks and bulges had appeared in the masonry. On Christmas Eve some repairs were carried out, but these clearly had not reduced the risk of collapse when the workers returned to work after Christmas.

A memorial to the victims of the disaster now stands at the junction of St Stephen's Road and Gaythorne Road. (A. Hall, *The Story of Bradford*)

22 April

Sir Jacob Behrens died on this date. Born near Hamburg in 1806, he came to Bradford in 1838, one of many German wool merchants who came to make their fortunes in the town.

Behrens was responsible for founding the Bradford Chamber of Commerce in 1851 and for the next thirty years – the heyday of the worsted trade in Bradford – German merchants accounted for about a quarter of the subscribers to the Chamber. In a tribute to Behrens on his death in 1889, the *Bradford Observer* commented: 'He was representative ... of the essentials, of the varied qualities which have made the town what it is commercially and socially.'

In another obituary, the *Illustrated Weekly Telegraph* said: 'Bradford is indebted to Behrens more than any other man for the bringing into life of the Chamber of Commerce and giving it not only importance among the mercantile community but weight and influence with the government on mercantile matters.'

Behrens received a knighthood in 1882 in recognition of his work in promoting exports and the influence he had in shaping the policies of the Board of Trade. He also realised that if Bradford's commercial success was to be sustained, its trade and industry had to be led by well-educated managers and, to this end, he was instrumental in reorganising Bradford Grammar School in 1871 and establishing Bradford Technical College in 1882. (B. Duckett (ed.), *The German Immigrants: Their Influence in 19th Century Bradford*)

13 April

On this day the bitter Manningham Mills strike, which had been on-going since the previous December, reached its climax. There had been a downturn in the textile export trade and the management at Manningham Mills sought to deal with this by reducing their employees' wages. Negotiations between workers and management quickly broke down and a strike ensued. Before long several thousand workers were involved. The winter was particularly harsh that year and many families suffered severe hardship.

There was a good deal of support for the strikers, but the city fathers, and the local Watch Committee in particular, tended to side with the employers, even to the point of attempting to ban strike meetings. Nevertheless, a demonstration in support of the strikers was called for 13 April. It attracted many hundreds of people to the centre of Bradford and violence broke out that evening. The mayor was compelled to read the Riot Act and troops with fixed bayonets were deployed to disperse the hostile crowds. Although many people (and some police horses) were injured, nobody was killed in the several hours of rioting. The strike itself ended later that month and the striking workers had to return to work on greatly reduced wages.

One important outcome of the strike was the creation in Bradford, two years later, of the Independent Labour Party. (C. Pearce, *The Manningham Mills Strike*)

6 September

Nobel Prize winner Edward Appleton was born in Bradford on this date. He attended Hanson School before going on to Cambridge University. He later served with the Royal Engineers in the First World War and began to develop an interest in radio. In 1924 he became Professor of Physics at King's College, London, and then Professor of Natural Philosophy at Cambridge.

Appleton conducted research into the field of radio and was particularly interested in the question of why radio waves behave in one way during daylight and in a different way after dark. He was able to confirm that radio waves were reflected back to earth by a heavily ionised layer – the ionosphere – in the upper atmosphere and that this layer was subject to changes due to the presence or absence of sunlight. He successfully identified a sub-division of the ionosphere, which became known as the Appleton layer. This was about 350 kilometres above the earth and was the first object ever to have been discovered solely by radio. Short-wave radio signals could be reflected from the Appleton layer and this opened up the possibility of round-the-world broadcasting. Most importantly, his work on radio waves paved the way for the development of radar.

In 1941, Appleton was knighted and he received the Nobel Prize for Physics in 1947. He died in 1965. (A. Hall, *The Story of Bradford*)

13 January

On this day the Independent Labour Party (ILP) was founded at a conference held at Firth's Temperance Hotel in Chapel Street. The creation of the ILP was a direct consequence of the Manningham Mills strike of 1890–91. Fred Jowett, who would be elected as Bradford's first ILP MP in 1906, summed up the rationale behind the founding of this new political party: 'In the Lister strike, the people of Bradford saw plainly, as they had never seen before, that whether their rulers are Liberal or Tory they are capitalists first and politicians afterwards.'

The first chairman of the ILP was Keir Hardie and Ramsay MacDonald was chairman from 1906 to 1909. MacDonald went on to become the United Kingdom's first Labour prime minister.

The party failed to gain any seats in Parliament in the 1895 general election and it was really only when it became an affiliate of the newly formed Labour Party in 1906 that it made much electoral headway. In Bradford itself the party made good progress and by 1914 it was polling more than 40 per cent of votes in local elections. Having gained some political influence, the party promoted a programme of improvements in Bradford, especially in housing, education and public health. It also encouraged the development of educational classes, cultural activities and social clubs, but after 1918 it declined, both nationally and locally. (C. Pearce, *The Manningham Mills Strike*; D. James, *Bradford*)

1894

13 September

John Boynton 'J.B.' Priestley was born today. He was educated at Belle Vue School, before working for a time in Swan Arcade for a firm of wool merchants. After serving in the First World War, he became a full-time writer. The publication of *The Good Companions* in 1929 made him famous, although nowadays his plays – such as *An Inspector Calls* and *When We Are Married* – are probably better known than his novels. During the Second World War, Priestley's Sunday evening radio broadcasts, 'Postscript', were very popular, though some people objected to his Yorkshire accent and his left-wing sympathies. Nevertheless, it was said that only Churchill's broadcasts commanded larger audiences.

Although Priestley enjoyed widespread popularity in Britain and abroad, his relationship with his native city was, especially in the 1950s and 1960s, not an easy one. Things came to a head in 1958 when he made a BBC television documentary entitled *Lost City*. Many people felt that not only had he deserted Bradford, he was now condemning it. Priestley defended himself by stating that the title was a nostalgic reference to the Bradford of his youth and was not meant to be a negative comment on the modern city. Eventually harmony was restored and Priestley was granted the freedom of the city of Bradford in 1973. He died in 1984. (P. Holdsworth, *The Rebel Tyke*)

9 June

On this day, eight years after becoming a county borough and on the fiftieth anniversary of its incorporation, Bradford was elevated to city status by Queen Victoria. Becoming a city was, in many ways, a symbolic gesture rather than anything else and it was duly accompanied by symbolic features. From 1907 onwards, for example, Bradford's leading citizen would be the lord mayor, rather than merely the mayor. Symbols are important and city status was particularly so, for it marked Bradford's quite remarkable progress. Throughout the nineteenth century, Bradford had grown at a phenomenal rate – faster possibly than any other place in Britain. In 1801 it had been little more than an obscure market town, with a population of about 6,000 people. By 1851 it had a population of 180,000 and had been for much of the intervening years a chaotic and unregulated place – perhaps even ungovernable. But by the last decades of the nineteenth century it had developed into a modern city of almost 300,000 people, and it had become the international centre of the wool trade. In 1910 it was estimated to be one of the wealthiest cities in Europe.

With its new status, Bradford had now become one of the great cities of the North, which were responsible – through their entrepreneurialism and industry – for making Victorian Britain the most prosperous and influential country in the world. (B. Duckett and J. Waddington-Feather, *Bradford, History & Guide*; A. Hall, *The Story of Bradford*; G. Firth, *A History of Bradford*)

4 May

On this day the Prince and Princess of Wales (the future King George V and Queen Mary) visited Bradford to officially open the Bradford Art and Industrial Exhibition in Lister Park. The ornate gates on North Park Road commemorate the visit. Later the same day, the prince and princess unveiled a statue of Queen Victoria in the centre of Bradford, and they attended a banquet at St George's Hall that evening.

The exhibition itself contained 145 individual displays positioned throughout Lister Park, including some in Cartwright Hall, which had been opened by Lord Masham (formerly Samuel Lister) less than a month before. Some buildings housing displays were temporary; one of these, the Industrial Hall, stood where the bowling greens are now.

The exhibition was open until the end of October, during which time there were almost 2.5 million visitors. Although the principal intention of the exhibition was to showcase Bradford's industries, especially its textiles, the most popular attractions had little or nothing to do with Bradford, and included the Somali village in which about 100 Somalis endured Bradford's uncertain climate for the duration of the exhibition. The Canadian Water Chute and the Crystal Maze also proved popular. William 'Buffalo Bill' Cody may or may not have appeared at the exhibition; certainly his Wild West Show had performed in Bradford in October 1903. (J. Appleby and J. Greenhalf, *Telegraph and Argus Stories of the Century*)

13 October

Sadly this day saw England's most famous actor of the time, Sir Henry Irving, collapse and die in the foyer of the Midland Hotel, Bradford, where he was staying. He had been appearing in the title role of *Beckett* at the Theatre Royal in Manningham Lane, just a few hundred yards from the hotel. During the performance it became clear to some members of the audience that Irving was unwell. His last line, perhaps appropriately, was 'Into thy hands ...' uttered just before the curtain fell on the final act of the play. His manager, Bram Stoker, best known as the author of *Dracula*, managed to get Irving to the Midland Hotel and was with him when he died. A battered suitcase, with Stoker's name on it, stands as an exhibit in one of the corridors of the hotel. A plaque commemorating Irving's death can be seen near to the hotel's main entrance, and facsimiles of press cuttings about Irving are also on display. Irving had appeared several times at the Theatre Royal, including playing opposite Ellen Terry in *The Merchant of Venice* in 1901.

The Theatre Royal became a cinema in 1921. It was renamed the Classic in 1967 and finally closed its doors in 1974. The building stood derelict until 1990 when it was demolished. The Midland Hotel, restored and refurbished in the 1990s, continues to flourish. (J. Appleby and J. Greenhalf, *Telegraph and Argus Stories of the Century*)

14 May

Charlie Chaplin, then aged 17, appeared at the Empire Theatre in Great Horton Road on this day. The Empire was Bradford's premier music hall, an imposing building with a lavishly appointed interior. Later the building became a cinema, and later still it was transformed into the Alexandra Hotel. It was demolished in 1993.

Chaplin appeared at the Empire on two more occasions, in 1909 and in 1910, as a leading member of Fred Karno's famous company. This was a vaudeville troupe, specialising in comic sketches and revues, and Chaplin was hugely popular in the role of Jimmy the Fearless.

Soon afterwards Chaplin left England, and from 1914 onwards he made a series of extremely successful silent films in the USA. By 1918 he was not just Hollywood's best-known film star, he was probably the most famous person on the planet.

In 1956, Chaplin returned to Bradford for a brief visit, '... to see if I could recapture some of the old days when I was touring'. By that time his fame had diminished. A series of scandals involving women in the 1940s, as well as accusations of left-wing sympathies, meant that Chaplin was forced to leave the USA. He settled in Switzerland. In his later years the US authorities relented and he received an Oscar in 1972. In Britain he was knighted in 1975. Chaplin died in 1977. (J. Appleby and J. Greenhalf, *Telegraph and Argus Stories of the Century*)

26 April

Bradford City defeated Newcastle United 1–0 at Old Trafford to win the FA Cup on this day. The match was a replay, the first match on 22 April at Crystal Palace having ended in a goalless draw. The winning goal was scored by Jimmy Speirs with a header in the fifteenth minute. The FA Cup itself was, coincidentally, designed and manufactured by the Bradford firm of jewellers, Fattorini & Sons, to replace an earlier trophy. Bradford City were the first holders of this new cup.

Bradford City were founded in 1903 when, with the encouragement of the Football Association and the Football League, it was decided that Manningham FC, a Rugby League club, would change codes to association football. The newly formed Bradford City took over Manningham's Valley Parade ground and their claret and amber club colours. After five years in the Second Division of the Football League, Bradford City were promoted to the First Division in 1908, winning the FA Cup just three years later. It could be said that this period prior to the First World War constituted the best days for a club that has never since won a major trophy. And, despite two comparatively recent seasons in the Premier League (1999–2001), Bradford City have usually played in the lower divisions of the English Football League. (J. Appleby and J. Greenhalf, *Telegraph and Argus Stories of the Century*)

20 June

This day saw Britain's first two municipally owned trolley bus services commence operations – one in Bradford, the other in Leeds. In Bradford the lord mayor, Jacob Moser, threw the switch to power the city's first trolley bus, which ran from Laisterdyke to Dudley Hill.

Trolley buses were seen as more economical for serving those areas where the population was too small to warrant the cost of providing a tramway service. They were also better than trams at tackling Bradford's steep hills. After 1914 no more tram routes were created, but in the same year a new trolley bus route was opened, linking Odsal and Oakenshaw. In the following year routes to Bolton Woods and Frizinghall commenced. Routes linking the city centre to the suburbs now opened at regular intervals; to Clayton (1926), to Allerton (1929), to Saltaire via Thackley (1930) and so on, right up to the 1950s, when routes to two large post-war council estates – Buttershaw and Holme Wood – became the final parts of Bradford's trolley bus network.

At its height, Bradford had a fleet of 200 trolley buses, but this had dwindled to 100 by 1967; the motor bus was proving to be more economical. Bradford's (and Britain's) last trolley bus made its final journey on 26 March 1972. Bradford had been the first and the last in the field. (J.S. King, *Bradford Corporation Trolleybuses*)

18 March

On this day the Alhambra Theatre first opened its doors to the public. Situated on a sloping site in Morley Street, it was named after the Alhambra Palace in Granada. Its design has some hints of Moorish architecture, in particular the large domed turrets on the roof, though the architects, Chadwick and Watson, preferred to describe it as 'English Renaissance of the Georgian period'. The Alhambra was built at a cost of £20,000 for the impresario Francis Laidler, who was known as 'The King of Pantomime', and right up to the present time the Alhambra has been regarded as one of the best places in the North of England to see a Christmas pantomime.

The Alhambra went through difficult times after Laidler died in 1955, and Bradford Council felt obliged to purchase it in the 1960s – at one point it was even scheduled for demolition to make room for a car park. However, especially since it was refurbished and extended in the 1980s (thanks largely to European funding), it has hosted major touring productions of all kinds, including those of the Royal Shakespeare Company and various prestigious West End shows, as well as its traditional pantomimes. The main auditorium now seats 1,400 and the smaller studio theatre has a capacity of 200 seated or 300 standing. It is a Grade 2 listed building. (G. Sheeran, *The Buildings of Bradford*; P. Leach and N. Pevsner, *The Buildings of England: Yorkshire West Riding*)

22 August

On this day the *Yorkshire Observer* reported that Brussels had fallen to the Germans, and the next day British and German troops clashed for the first time at Mons. These events led to some nasty incidents involving Bradford's German community. In the Manchester Road area, several German pork butcher shops had their windows broken, and in Keighley the Riot Act had to be read when a mob went on the rampage and attacked several German shops and businesses.

All people of German nationality in Bradford had been registered by 20 August; from that date they were denied the use of a motorcar or a telephone and their mail was carefully scrutinised. Soon afterwards many of them were arrested and interned on the Isle of Man for the duration. Others had already returned to Germany before war was declared on 4 August.

The German merchant community had not only enriched Bradford's commercial life before the war; it had also been instrumental in promoting the city's cultural and civic life, turning Bradford, in the opinion of many commentators, from a wholly provincial place into a city which had a more European and cosmopolitan character. Most of this was lost after 1914, and the leavening which the German community had given to Bradford largely disappeared, leaving the city a meaner place, according to some. (M. Woods and T. Platts, *Bradford in the Great War*; D. Raw, *Bradford Pals*)

25 June

Fred Hoyle was born in Bingley on this date. Educated at Bingley Grammar School and Cambridge University, Hoyle is known best for rejecting the so-called Big Bang theory of the origin of the universe in favour of his own steady-state theory, which proposed that the universe has always existed. He acknowledged that the universe was expanding, but he theorised that as the galaxies got further apart others developed to fill the space. He also developed a theory that the chemical elements could have their origin in the hot interiors of stars. Many of his colleagues in the scientific fraternity believed that he should have received a Nobel Prize for this work.

In 1958, Hoyle became Professor of Astrophysics and Natural Philosophy at Cambridge University and in 1966 he founded the Institute of Theoretical Astronomy. However, he clashed with some members of the university's hierarchy, and in 1972 he resigned his professorship and the chairmanship of the institute in order to pursue his work without constraint. From 1969 to 1971 he was vice president of the Royal Society and in 1972 he was knighted.

Hoyle was an excellent communicator and keen to keep the general public informed about scientific issues through radio broadcasts, popular scientific books and over a dozen science-fiction novels. He died in 2001. (A. Hall, *The Story of Bradford*)

1 July

On this day the two battalions of the Bradford Pals went into action on the first day of the catastrophic Battle of the Somme. Both battalions suffered horrendous casualties in a futile and badly planned attack. Many men were mown down by German machine guns as soon as they left their trenches. Every officer in the First Pals Battalion was either killed or wounded.

The Bradford Pals battalions were comprised of volunteers who had eagerly offered their services when war was declared two years earlier. These volunteers were largely from Bradford's class of white-collar workers – clerks, foremen, managers and professionals of various kinds – precisely the group which, given normal peacetime conditions, would have been expected to fill leading positions in Bradford's commercial, cultural and civic life. The loss, therefore, of this large group of Bradford's 'brightest and best' meant that the city had a reduced pool of talent to draw on once peace was restored in 1918. Some historians believe that Britain as a whole suffered from such a reduced pool of talent, and that to this day the country has never fully recovered from the Battle of the Somme. There were 60,000 casualties just on the first disastrous day of the battle.

Memorials to the Pals stand in the centre of Bradford and in the village of Hébuterne in northern France, close to where so many Pals fell that day. (M. Woods and T. Platts, *Bradford in the Great War*; D. Raw, *Bradford Pals*)

21 August

A wartime catastrophe occurred on the home front at this time. What we would now call an industrial estate existed at Low Moor, comprised of the Low Moor Iron Company, the Bradford Corporation Gas Works and the Low Moor Chemical Company, which produced lyddite, one of the main explosives used by the Royal Artillery.

That afternoon a drum of picric acid burst into flames as it was being moved in the chemical company's premises. The fire quickly spread and, about fifteen minutes later, there was a gigantic explosion, which was so loud that it was heard in Pateley Bridge, over 30 miles away. The chemical works' own firefighters were tackling the blaze when the explosion occurred. All were killed. Debris was scattered over a 1 mile radius.

As the first fire engine from Bradford arrived on the scene there was a second huge explosion. This killed six firemen and injured several others. A third explosion was caused when a gasholder of the Corporation Gas Works was ignited. There were more than twenty further explosions that afternoon and evening. Fires burned on the site for the next two days.

Householders in nearby Low Moor and Wyke fled, some spending the next two nights in local woods. A total of thirty-eight people lost their lives. An investigation concluded that the disaster was a tragic accident. (M. Woods and T. Platts, *Bradford in the Great War*; D. Raw, *Bradford Pals*)

25 November

On this day the diocese of Bradford was created and the parish church of St Peter became a cathedral. The new diocese stretched from Bradford itself up through the Yorkshire Dales as far as Sedbergh, which is now in Cumbria. The first Bishop of Bradford was Arthur Perowne.

Records show that in 1281 there was certainly a church on the present site of the cathedral, and it is likely that there was an earlier place of worship that may have been destroyed soon after the Norman Conquest. By the fourteenth century a stone church had been built, possibly to replace one burned down by marauding Scots who, after their victory at Bannockburn in 1314, frequently raided the North of England with impunity.

After the Reformation, Bradford had a series of Puritan vicars and the town developed a strong tradition of religious dissent, which flourished up to the nineteenth century and beyond. During the Civil War the parish church was used as a defensive stronghold when the Royalists besieged Bradford in 1642 and 1643.

In July 2013 it was decided to abolish the diocese of Bradford. A new diocese, centred on Leeds, was created to cover much of West and North Yorkshire. In February 2014 it was announced that the bishop of this new diocese would be Nick Baines, erstwhile Bishop of Bradford. (A. Hall, *The Story of Bradford*)

19 August

On this day two young girls, Elsie Wright and Frances Griffiths, took three photographs which seemed to show fairies cavorting near the beck at Cottingley, not far from Bingley. They had been encouraged to take the photographs by Edward Gardner of the Theosophical Society and Sir Arthur Conan Doyle, the creator of Sherlock Holmes. Conan Doyle was a firm believer in spiritualism. The girls had taken two similar photographs in the summer of 1917, and when these became public in 1919 the phenomenon of the 'Cottingley Fairies' became widely known and discussed.

Conan Doyle wrote an article for *The Strand Magazine* in December 1920 entitled, 'Evidence for Fairies', and he later wrote a book, *The Coming of the Fairies*. Well-known people, including the educationalist Margaret McMillan, also declared a belief that the photographs were genuine. Others were more sceptical, and in 1965, Elsie eventually admitted that the photographs had been faked, using cut-out pictures of fairies taken from children's books.

Why were eminent people like Conan Doyle and McMillan taken in by the girls' photographs? At the time interest in the paranormal was particularly widespread. It could be that the huge loss of life in the First World War had created a strong desire to believe in supernatural phenomena and a life beyond the grave. (F.M. Griffith and C. Lynch, *Reflections on the Cottingley Fairies*)

5 October

Work was commenced on Scar House Reservoir in upper Nidderdale on this day, to address a problem from which Bradford had suffered for a century – a shortage of water. Some progress had been made in the nineteenth century to ensure a better supply and Angram Reservoir had been built between 1904 and 1919. Despite this, the problem persisted. Alderman Anthony Gadie, whose brainchild Scar House had been, cut the first sod, but it was not until 1936 that the reservoir became operative. It cost over £8 million to construct. The reservoir dam, 71 metres high, was for some years the highest masonry dam in Europe.

Gadie (1868–1948) was primarily a builder, and he had been responsible in 1910 for what was known as 'Gadie's Garden Suburb' in Allerton. By the twentieth century, places like Allerton, on the outskirts of Bradford, had become more accessible by public transport. Better-off families therefore began to move away from the heavily polluted central areas of Bradford to healthier and more salubrious suburban neighbourhoods.

Gadie came in for criticism during the construction of Scar House. Some believed the project was far too expensive and dismissed it as 'Gadie's Folly'. However, severe droughts in 1933 and 1934 made people realise that Scar House was very necessary if Bradford was to overcome the problem of water shortage. Gadie was knighted in 1935. (A. Hall, *The Story of Bradford*; G. Firth, *A History of Bradford*)

13 April

The novelist John Braine was born near to St Patrick's church in White Abbey on this date. In *Memoirs* (1991) his friend Kingsley Amis wrote the following about him: '... his dream of real success was of a triumphal procession through Bradford with himself at the head, flanked by a pair of naked beauties draped with jewellery.'

It is perhaps this image of success that underlies his most famous novel, *Room at the Top*. Published in 1957, the book became an overnight sensation and a best-seller. It describes the class-based tensions within English society. The anti-hero, Joe Lampton, is a bright but penniless product of the working class, who believes that the only way to get to the top is by cynically exploiting every opportunity, including marrying the daughter of a wealthy local industrialist after getting her pregnant.

A film of the book, starring Laurence Harvey and Simone Signoret (who won an Oscar for her performance), was made in 1959. Much of it was shot on location in Bradford

Room at the Top led to Braine being categorised as a left-wing 'Angry Young Man', but before long he had moved to the far right in his politics, even supporting the apartheid regime in South Africa. He wrote about a dozen other books, but none had the impact (or the quality) of *Room at the Top*. Braine died in 1986. (A. Hall, *The Story of Bradford*)

1 July

On this day Bradford's principal war memorial, which stands in the centre of the city, was unveiled. Fittingly, the date was the sixth anniversary of the first day of the Somme offensive, when the two battalions of the Bradford Pals went into action in a futile attempt to capture the heavily fortified village of Serre on the Western Front. Hundreds of Bradford men were killed on that day.

The memorial obelisk is about 20 feet high and made of local stone, with the customary *Pro Patria Mori* inscribed near the top (unintentionally hinting at what Wilfred Owen famously called 'the old lie' in his poem 'Dulce et Decorum Est') At either side of the obelisk, as you face it, are two larger-than-life bronze figures, a soldier and a sailor, holding rifles in warlike poses. Originally the pair had fixed bayonets, but apparently this was deemed to be too uncomfortable an image – too violent perhaps to commemorate all those who were slaughtered in a war – so the bayonets had to be removed. They are replaced, however, every year on 11 November when the Remembrance Day ceremony is held at the memorial.

In January 2014 a second memorial nearby was dedicated to those armed forces personnel who, since 1945, have lost their lives on active service. (A. Hall, *The Story of Bradford*)

26 April

On this day, Ernest Busby opened his 'Store with the Friendly Welcome' on Manningham Lane, opposite the Theatre Royal. It became probably the most well-loved department store in Bradford. Originally a linen draper's apprentice in London, Busby had worked in Liverpool before coming to Bradford, no doubt attracted by the city's status as the wool capital of the world. He opened his first shop in Kirkgate on 5 October 1908; the crowd of eager shoppers had to be controlled by the police on that opening day.

The move to Manningham Lane meant that Busby's could now become a fully fledged department store. It expanded several times between 1931 and 1939 as its popularity grew. A restaurant was opened, followed by a laundry and later even a petrol service station for those customers with motorcars. Staff numbers increased from 150 to 800. After the Second World War, an ice-cream factory was added, and the nearby Fountain Hall was opened for functions and formal dinners.

Busby's was taken over by Debenhams in 1958, just one year after Ernest Busby died. The Busby name was retained for a time, but then dropped, and in 1978 Debenhams announced that the store would close and be demolished. There was a public outcry in Bradford. A few months later, in 1979, the now empty and semi-derelict building was totally destroyed by fire. (*Telegraph and Argus*, 2007)

22 September

This date saw Bradford's lord mayor, Alderman Angus Rhodes, open the New Victoria Cinema on the site of the former Whittaker's brewery in the centre of Bradford. Designed in an Italian classical style by the Bradford architect William Illingworth, the 3,500-capacity cinema auditorium was reckoned to be the largest in Britain outside London. The opening ceremony naturally included a showing of some of the latest films, notably the British comedy *Rookery Nook* and a Mickey Mouse cartoon entitled *Barnyard Concert*. An important feature of the auditorium was its excellent acoustics – many older cinemas had poor acoustics, but the New Victoria's auditorium had been specifically designed with talking pictures in mind. The building also contained a well-appointed restaurant and a ballroom.

In 1950 the cinema became the Gaumont. Because of its audience capacity, the Gaumont was also used as a concert venue, hosting a range of world-famous performers, especially in the 1950s and 1960s. For example, Beniamino Gigli appeared in 1954, Bill Haley and the Comets in 1957 and Buddy Holly in 1958, to be followed by such acts as The Beatles, the Rolling Stones and the Everly Brothers in the early 1960s.

In 1969 the cinema changed its name again and became the Odeon. Instead of one large auditorium, the available space was now split into several smaller cinemas.

The Odeon closed in 2000. (G. Sheeran, *The Buildings of Bradford*; P. Leach and N. Pevsner, *The Buildings of England: Yorkshire West Riding*)

13 July

HRH Prince George, Duke of Kent, formally opened a week-long extravaganza in Peel Park entitled 'The Historical Pageant of Bradford' on this day. This 'Living Story of Bradford's Glory' involved 7,500 performers dressed in costumes from various periods in Bradford's history. As Bradford has very little history to speak of prior to the Industrial Revolution, one might wonder why some performers were dressed as medieval peasants, Roman soldiers and even ancient Britons, or indeed what Robin Hood had to do with Bradford.

Nevertheless, the pageant attracted large crowds. Lloyd George turned up one day and delivered a speech to an audience of 12,000 people. Many of the dramatized historical scenes were written by well-known Yorkshire writers, such as Phyllis Bentley. In addition, there was an orchestra of 150 musicians, a chorus of 500 singers and a children's choir of 300. It was estimated that 30,000 people (one-tenth of Bradford's population) had been involved in some way or other in the production of the pageant.

The pageant was intended to complement the Imperial Wool Industries Fair, which was being held that same week at Olympia Hall in Thornton Road. This was designed to showcase Bradford's textile trade, which was going through difficulties in 1931. As J.B. Priestley remarked, the pageant helped to cheer people up at a time of growing uncertainty about the future. (J. Appleby and J. Greenhalf, *Telegraph and Argus Stories of the Century*)

17 October

Leeds and Bradford Airport, then called Yeadon Aerodrome, began operating on a 60-acre grassland site next to the main Bradford–Harrogate road. At first it functioned only as a flying club, but in 1935 a few scheduled passenger flights to places like Newcastle, Blackpool and the Isle of Man were inaugurated.

During the Second World War all civilian flights ceased and the aerodrome was used by military aircraft, including those built at the adjacent Avro factory; over 5,000 military aircraft, including about 700 Lancasters, were built there.

Civilian flights started again in 1947 and from that time onward the airport expanded considerably. By the late twentieth century it was capable of handling even the largest aircraft for intercontinental flights.

The airport was originally jointly owned by Bradford and Leeds councils, but in 2007 it was sold to Bridgepoint Capital who continued to expand the airport's facilities and the number of destinations served. It is estimated that by 2016 the airport will handle over 5 million passengers per annum.

Leeds Bradford Airport is the highest in England at 681 feet above sea level; essentially it sits on a plateau along the top of Otley Chevin. This can have its drawbacks, as hill fogs sometimes form, especially in autumn, and the airport can be affected by high winds and snow during the winter months. (www.leedsbradfordairport.co.uk)

22 May

Many inhabitants of Bradford watched as the German airship *Hindenburg* flew over the city on its way from Lakehurst, New Jersey, to Frankfurt in Germany. Hitler and the Nazis had been in power in Germany since 1933, and the large swastika, which adorned the airship, could easily be seen by those on the ground.

To many watchers the airship seemed to be flying particularly low and soon there were rumours that it was on some kind of aerial spying mission in preparation for a future war. However, its low altitude over Keighley may have been to facilitate the dropping of a wreath of carnations and a crucifix. These were to be placed on the graves of German prisoners of war who were buried in Morton Cemetery, between Keighley and Bingley. These prisoners had survived the First World War only to become victims, in 1919, of the influenza epidemic that swept through many countries, killing millions of people.

The *Hindenburg* was 808 feet long, 135 feet in diameter and cruised at the relatively slow speed of 76mph, making it clearly visible for some time as it flew across Bradford. On 6 May 1937 it abruptly burst into flames as it was docking at Lakehurst and thirty-five of its ninety-seven passengers and crew were killed. This marked the end of the transatlantic airship era. (J. Appleby and J. Greenhalf, *Telegraph and Argus Stories of the Century*)

1 December

On this day the *Bradford Telegraph and Argus* reported a speech that the Bishop of Bradford, Dr Alfred Blunt, had delivered about the forthcoming coronation of King Edward VIII. In the speech the bishop referred to the new king's 'need for grace'. This was quickly interpreted as a criticism of Edward's affair with Wallace Simpson, although the bishop was later to state that this was not his intention and that, in common with many people at the time, he had never even heard of Mrs Simpson. Rather, Blunt said, his words were meant to indicate a concern that Edward seemed indifferent to the Church of England, even though, as monarch, he was supposed to be at its head. Whilst Blunt may have been unaware of Edward's affair with Mrs Simpson, others were not; there had been growing concerns in government circles about the couple's relationship, especially as Mrs Simpson was a divorcee and so any future marriage to Edward could not be sanctioned by the Church of England.

Whatever the bishop's actual intentions may have been, his words were soon seized upon by the national press and then the general public. Within a fortnight, Edward had abdicated the throne in favour of his brother George. Edward and Mrs Simpson subsequently became the Duke and Duchess of Windsor; they lived abroad for the remainder of their lives. (J. Appleby and J. Greenhalf, *Telegraph and Argus Stories of the Century*)

1937

19 July

David Hockney was born on this date. He is Britain's best-known contemporary artist. Brought up in Eccleshill, he was educated at Bradford Grammar School, after which he attended Bradford Art College. There he sold his first picture, a portrait of his father, for which he received £10. Hockney may also have painted some murals to decorate the walls of the nearby Alassio coffee bar, a favourite haunt of Bradford's art students and bohemians at that time.

Hockney left Bradford to study at the Royal College of Art, where his reputation as a highly talented and innovative artist started to grow. In 1964 he moved to the USA and his reputation grew further. His series of paintings featuring Californian swimming pools became internationally famous, and in 1974 one of them, *A Bigger Splash*, provided the title for a film about Hockney's life and work.

In the later part of the twentieth century, Hockney started to produce photo collages, and he also made much use of fax machines, digital cameras and other technological equipment to produce his art. His works appear in galleries throughout the world. Hockney has always maintained a connection with Bradford, and Salts Mill houses the 1853 Gallery – an impressive collection of his work. In January 2012 he was awarded the Order of Merit, having previously declined a knighthood. (A. Hall, *The Story of Bradford*)

31 August

On this day Bradford experienced its only serious air raid of the Second World War. There were three air raids on Bradford that August. The first took place on the night of 22 August, when three bombs were dropped harmlessly into Heaton Woods. Six days later, there was another raid. There were no casualties and little damage was done, though St Peter's church in Leeds Road was hit and so were several shops.

On 31 August, German aircraft were over Bradford from about a quarter-past eleven until almost three o'clock the next morning. About 120 bombs in total were dropped causing significant damage to the city. Only one, or possibly two, people were killed, although over 100 were injured.

Lingards drapery store was destroyed, as was part of Rawson Market and a mill in Nelson Street. The Odeon cinema, then at the bottom of Manchester Road, was hit; fortunately the audience had left. An incendiary bomb landed in Wapping School swimming pool and was thus immediately extinguished, although a nearby factory, which produced sulphuric acid, was less fortunate and was partially destroyed. Maps captured from the Germans after the war seemed to indicate that the principal target for the raid may have been the Phoenix engineering works at Thornbury. No further air raids of any significance were made on Bradford during the war. (A. Hall, *The Story of Bradford*)

26 March

King George VI and Queen Elizabeth paid a morale-boosting visit to Bradford on this day. For reasons of security the visit was kept secret until the actual day. Likewise, the mill that the royal couple visited to see uniforms being made was never identified in the press. It was possibly Lister's Mill, although most of the wartime production there had been turned over to the manufacture of silk for parachutes and a rubber substitute called Resilitex, which was used for camouflage purposes.

Later in the day, the king and queen inspected 700 Civil Defence workers and 300 National Fire Service members in Lister Park, before finally heading out to Steeton to visit the Royal Ordnance factory there. Two-thirds of the workers at this factory were women and during the war they produced 63 million shells.

Buckingham Palace suffered bomb damage during the blitz on London, and the government suggested that the royal family should move to Canada for safety, but the king and queen insisted on staying in England. For this they were generally admired during the war.

The couple had visited Bradford on one previous occasion, in April 1928, when they were the Duke and Duchess of York. And when she was Queen Mother, Elizabeth returned to the city in March 1962 to attend the Delius Centenary Festival at St George's Hall. (J. Appleby and J. Greenhalf, *Telegraph and Argus Stories of the Century*)

1 February

Fred Jowett died on this date, one day after his eightieth birthday. In 1892 he was the first socialist to be elected to Bradford Council and for the next fifteen years he sought, with some success, to persuade Bradford's civic leaders to carry out various pioneering social reforms. He also worked alongside Margaret McMillan to promote better education and welfare for children.

Improving housing conditions for the poor was one of his main concerns, and in 1909, Bradford's first municipal housing scheme was completed. Jowett's legacy was the Longlands Improvement Area, situated in Goitside, to rehouse families from the Goitside and White Abbey slums. The council cleared slum properties and erected five blocks of three-storey tenements in Longlands Street, following these with more in Chain Street and Roundhill Place.

The Housing Act of 1919 gave councils financial incentives to build houses and Bradford Corporation responded by building more than 10,000 council houses between then and the outbreak of the Second World War. That figure represented almost 50 per cent of the houses built in the city in that period.

Jowett was one of the founder members of the Independent Labour Party and became the MP for Bradford West in 1906. For a short period in 1924 he served as a minister in Ramsay Macdonald's first Labour administration. (A. Hall, *The Story of Bradford*)

3 May

On this day Bradford Northern beat their great rivals Leeds to win the Rugby League Challenge Cup at Wembley Stadium. The score was 8–4. Leeds had started as favourites to win the final, having progressed through the earlier rounds without conceding a single point. However, on the day, Bradford Northern proved to be the better side and the team's stand-off half, the Welsh international Willie Davis, was particularly outstanding. He won the Lance Todd Trophy as Man of the Match. On returning to Bradford the victorious team drove through the city on an open-topped bus before joining the lord mayor for a civic reception at the Town Hall.

The 1940s were halcyon days for Bradford Northern. They won the Yorkshire Cup on five occasions and returned to Wembley in 1948, but were beaten by Wigan 8–3 in that year's Challenge Cup Final. The following year, however, they defeated Halifax 12–0 to win the cup. The 1948 match was notable for being the first Rugby League Final attended by a reigning monarch, George VI. It was also the first match to be televised – not that many people had television sets at that time.

Bradford Northern became Bradford Bulls when Super League was formed in 1996. In the early years of the new competition the Bulls were champions six times and world champions on three occasions. (J. Appleby and J. Greenhalf, *Telegraph and Argus Stories of the Century*)

16 June

On this day the *Telegraph and Argus* reported that a Jowett Jupiter sports car, manufactured at Jowett's factory in Idle, had left Bradford to compete in the famous Le Mans 24-Hour Grand Prix. The Jupiter went on to win its class at Le Mans in three successive years, as well as winning the 1.5-litre class at the 1951 Monte Carlo Rally. Despite these successes the Jupiter failed to make much impact with the car-buying public; only 1,000 were ever manufactured.

Ben and Willie Jowett started building motorcars in 1906 at a workshop in Manningham; their factory in Idle was opened in 1920. In 1927, Scotland Yard purchased a fleet of Jowett cars, and in 1947 the firm began to produce its most successful model, the Jowett Javelin which, like the Jupiter, enjoyed success in its class at the Monte Carlo Rally. A total of 23,000 Javelins were produced between 1947 and 1953.

However, Jowett, with its tradition of making quality cars that were largely hand-built, never really adjusted in the post-war era to the rapidly growing market for mass-produced, cheap family cars. In 1954 the factory at Idle was sold to International Harvester, which operated there until the early 1980s. After that the factory was demolished and the Idle site became a retail park, dominated by a large Wm Morrison supermarket. (J. Appleby and J. Greenhalf, *Telegraph and Argus Stories of the Century*)

5 May

This day saw more than 102,000 spectators attend the replay of the Rugby League Challenge Cup Final at Odsal Stadium. In fact, because many people gatecrashed the match, it is likely that the actual attendance was closer to 120,000 – in any case it was the largest crowd ever to have attended a Rugby League match in Britain. The official attendance at Odsal stood as a world record until the 1999 National Rugby League Grand Final attracted a crowd of 107,000 to Stadium Australia.

The match at Odsal was between Warrington and Halifax. These teams had drawn 4–4 at Wembley – incidentally the only Challenge Cup Final when no tries were scored – and the Odsal replay ended with Warrington the victors by 8–4. Both games were widely regarded to have been drab affairs.

Odsal Stadium was opened in 1934, on a site which had previously been a quarry and later Bradford's major refuse tip; the stadium bankings were formed out of 140,000 cart-loads of household waste. Often touted as a possible 'Wembley of the North', the stadium has never been properly developed to fulfil its potential as a major sporting venue. However, it has hosted speedway, baseball, basketball, show jumping, tennis and live music concerts. After the tragic fire of 1985, Bradford City played some of their home fixtures at Odsal Stadium until Valley Parade was reopened. (J. Appleby and J. Greenhalf, *Telegraph and Argus Stories of the Century*)

26 November

In the evening of 26 November, fighting broke out between rival gangs of so-called Teddy Boys outside the Ideal Ballroom in Bankfoot. Trouble had started earlier inside the ballroom when rival gangs from Bradford and Keighley began to scuffle in the balcony area. Before long the violence spilled out into the street and a crowd of about 200 people – some participants in the fighting, others merely onlookers – blocked Manchester Road, one of the city's busiest roads. The crowd only dispersed after a baton charge by the police.

Seventeen young men were subsequently given short prison sentences and fourteen more were fined or bound over. Several knives, razors and knuckle-dusters were seized by the police. Three girls, not at all involved in the fighting, were caught up in the melee and suffered stab wounds that required hospital treatment. No policemen were reported injured, though several police helmets were damaged.

Teddy Boy violence was a topical issue at the time, often rather hysterically reported in the popular press. The reality was that fighting on a Saturday night between groups of usually inebriated young men was nothing new in large towns and cities such as Bradford. As early as 1851 the *Bradford Observer* had noted incidents of 'faction fighting' – mass brawls between rival gangs, especially within Bradford's Irish community. (J. Appleby and J. Greenhalf, *Telegraph and Argus Stories of the Century*)

3 March

On this day one of the handsomest of Bradford's Victorian buildings, Swan Arcade, closed its doors for the last time. The next day demolition commenced. Swan Arcade had opened in 1879 on the site of the old White Swan Inn and housed up-market retailers, such as a cigar shop and high-class tailors. Its office space was mainly occupied by firms of wool brokers and the like. J.B. Priestley was employed by one of these for a time when he left school, and although he found the work rather dull, he admired Swan Arcade itself. When it became clear that the building was under threat of demolition, Priestley campaigned vigorously to save it, but to no avail. In fact, many Bradford citizens felt that Priestley had abandoned his native city years before and so his opinion did not really count for much.

Besides, Stanley Wardley, the city engineer, had devised an ambitious modernisation scheme. This involved tearing down many of the Victorian buildings in the city centre and replacing them with edifices that were supposedly more in keeping with the modern age. Thus it was that, on 10 December 1963, Yorkshire and England fast bowler Fred Trueman ceremonially topped out Arndale House, generally viewed as a vastly inferior replacement for Swan Arcade. Perhaps Trueman should have stuck to cricket. (J. Appleby and J. Greenhalf, *Telegraph and Argus Stories of the Century*)

2 February

On this day The Beatles made their first visit to Bradford to perform at the Gaumont cinema (later to become the Odeon). At this stage in their career they were not the top of the bill; that honour went to the young female singer, Helen Shapiro. The Beatles returned to the Gaumont on 21 December 1963, this time as the top act, and they also commenced their 1964 UK tour at the Gaumont on 9 October 1964. Tickets to see them on this last occasion were priced from 10s 6d to 17s 6d – quite expensive for those days – and The Beatles themselves received a fee of £850 for the show, which nowadays seems rather modest.

In the mid-1960s The Beatles vied with the Rolling Stones as the UK's most popular and significant group. The Rolling Stones first appeared at the Gaumont a few months after The Beatles had paid their initial visit. On that occasion, on 19 October 1963, the Stones were a support act to the Everly Brothers, who topped the bill. Bo Diddley also appeared that night. Two years later, on 4 October 1965, the Rolling Stones appeared at the Gaumont again. This time, as befitted a band who had by now become famous throughout the world, they were the top of the bill. (J. Appleby and J. Greenhalf, *Telegraph and Argus Stories of the Century*)

25 April

On this day Jim Fryatt, playing for Bradford Park Avenue, scored the fastest goal ever recorded in an English Football League match. Fryatt had the ball in Tranmere Rovers' net just four seconds after the kick-off.

Bradford Park Avenue (simply called 'Bradford' for most of their history and generally referred to as 'Avenue' in the Bradford area) were formed in 1907 and elected to the Football League the following year. Like their traditional rivals, Bradford City, the club originally played rugby. Some breakaway members of the club stuck with Rugby League and founded Bradford Northern, later to be renamed Bradford Bulls.

The club's name is derived from their original home ground, which was on Horton Park Avenue in Little Horton. The football stadium adjoined what was once one of Yorkshire County Cricket Club's principal venues; the last first-class cricket match was played there in 1996. Professional football also ceased to be played at Park Avenue when the club dropped out of the Football League and went into liquidation in the 1970s. Reborn shortly afterwards, initially as a Sunday league side, Bradford Park Avenue steadily progressed until, by the early years of the twenty-first century, they were in Conference North, the sixth tier of the English Football League system. The club currently plays at Horsfall Stadium in Odsal, but has retained its traditional name. (B. Hugman, *Football League Players Records*)

29 June

The Keighley and Worth Valley Railway, one of Britain's most well-known heritage railways, opened to the public on this date. The line had originally opened in 1867, financed by local mill owners. They saw a need for the growing number of textile mills in Haworth, Oxenhope and Oakworth to be serviced by a railway, which would be linked to the rail network at Keighley.

The line was closed in 1962 as part of the cuts orchestrated by Dr Beeching. The Keighley and Worth Valley Railway Preservation Society was set up soon afterwards, with Bob Cryer (who was Keighley's MP from 1974 to 1983) as its first chair. The society duly purchased the line from British Rail over a period of twenty-five years, and in 1968 the railway began to operate again – this time staffed wholly by volunteer railway enthusiasts.

The line runs for 5 miles along the Worth Valley from Keighley to Haworth and Oxenhope. It has become a major tourist attraction, especially when steam locomotives are used to pull the trains. The railway currently carries over 100,000 passengers a year.

Film-makers have made good use of the railway for period pieces since its reopening. In 1970 the feature film *The Railway Children* used the line as a location, and Bob Cryer himself had a small role, playing the part of a railway guard. (R. Povey, *The History of the Keighley and Worth Valley Railway*)

30 May

Ian Clough was killed by a falling ice-pillar on the lower slopes of Annapurna in the Himalayas on this date. He was a member of Chris Bonnington's expedition, which had successfully made the ascent of the south face of Annapurna. Clough was killed on the lower slopes during the descent of the mountain. Bonnington dedicated his book *Annapurna South Face* (1971) to Clough.

Clough was born in Baildon in 1937 and became one of the finest climbers of his generation. He practised some of his climbing techniques on Baildon Bank, an old quarry rock face, 50 feet high, which looks out towards the centre of Bradford. He climbed extensively in Britain and abroad, and made the first ascent of the Central Pillar of Frêney on Mont Blanc in 1961. The following year, with Bonnington, he made the first successful ascent by a British team of the north face of the Eiger. Clough's wife Niki was also a climber and they climbed the north face of the Matterhorn together.

Ian Clough Hall was established in the centre of Baildon as a memorial to Clough shortly after his death. The hall functions as a community centre and an arts venue. A brass plaque in Clough's memory was erected at Annapurna base camp in 1999 and an earlier memorial is nearby, cut into the rock of the mountain. (C. Bonnington, *Annapurna South Face*; D. Lister, *Bradford's Own*)

1974

1 April

On this day local government throughout England was radically changed. Bradford became the principal partner in a newly created metropolitan district, which stretched from the city itself almost to Skipton on the edge of the Yorkshire Dales. Towns such as Keighley and Ilkley, which had always relished their independence, were now somewhat unwillingly subsumed into this new administrative unit, along with smaller places such as Denholme and Queensbury. The new district consisted of eleven former authorities in all.

Several bizarre suggestions for a name for this new authority were mooted, including Wharfeaire and Broadmoor. Finally the City of Bradford Metropolitan District was chosen. This name may have satisfied the people of Bradford itself, but it was hardly going to be popular elsewhere. The new Bradford Council had ninety members and there was a new coat of arms, made up of bits of the arms of the eleven former authorities. A new motto was introduced, 'Progress, Industry, Humanity', which replaced Bradford's original *Labor Omnia Vincit*.

The new regime favoured a modern corporate management approach, which from now on would emanate from the chief executive's office in the centre of Bradford. How effective the new arrangements would be in helping Bradford to face up to the challenges of the future, nobody could tell. For some critics, the fact that the new regime had commenced on All Fools' Day said it all. (A. Hall, *The Story of Bradford*)

24 May

On this day, Bradford boxer Richard Dunn (born 1945) fought Muhammad Ali, formerly Cassius Clay, for the WBA/WBC World Heavyweight boxing title. The fight took place at the Olympiahalle in Munich. Despite being knocked down five times by Ali, Dunn fought courageously until the referee stopped the fight in the fifth round; Ali had won by a technical knockout. It is said that Ali had written 'Ali wins' inside one of his gloves and 'Round five' in the other, thus accurately predicting his victory. It was in fact the last time that Ali won a fight with a knockout.

In his next fight, in October 1976, Dunn was knocked out in the first round by Joe Bugner and so relinquished his British, Commonwealth and European titles. He retired the following year after one final fight in South Africa, where he was knocked out by Kallie Knoetze. In the twenty-first century, Dunn was living in retirement in Scarborough on the Yorkshire coast.

Despite his being defeated by Ali, Bradfordians were proud of Dunn's achievement in challenging the world champion, so when, in 1978, a new leisure facility was constructed in Rooley Avenue, it was named the Richard Dunn Sports Centre. Sadly, in September 2013, Bradford Council announced that it planned to close the centre, along with several municipal swimming pools, as part of its cost-cutting strategy. (D. Lister, *Bradford's Own*)

27 February

Bradford's most prestigious department store, Brown Muff, the 'Harrods of the North', ceased to exist from this date. For a time, a branch of Rackham's traded from the Brown Muff building in Market Street, but this closed in 1995. The building is still there, now divided up into a variety of retail outlets.

Brown Muff could trace its history back to 1814, when a widow, Elizabeth Brown, opened a clothes shop on Market Street. Later the shop was taken over by Elizabeth's son, Henry, who soon went into partnership with his brother-in-law, Thomas Muff.

The original shop was replaced in 1870 by the present building, and over the ensuing decades Brown Muff became a fully fledged, upmarket department store. At the height of its prestige, the store attracted well-heeled customers from far beyond Bradford.

By the twentieth century the store was owned by the Muff family, who lived in Ilkley. In 1909 the family changed its name to Maufe, thus provoking the following somewhat sardonic rhyme:

> In Bradford 'tis good enough
> To be known as Mrs Muff,
> But in Ilkley by the River Wharfe
> It's better to be known as Mrs Maufe.

In 1917 Thomas Harold Maufe, a son of the family, was awarded the Victoria Cross. He survived the First World War, but was killed in an accident whilst training with the Home Guard in 1942. (*Telegraph and Argus*, 2010)

2 January

In the late evening of 2 January, Peter Sutcliffe, the so-called Yorkshire Ripper, was arrested in Sheffield. He eventually confessed to the murder of thirteen women. Sutcliffe was born in Shipley, brought up in Bingley and was living in the Heaton area of Bradford when he was arrested.

Sutcliffe murdered Wilma McCann in Leeds in October 1975. Between that killing and his arrest, Sutcliffe murdered at least another ten women in West Yorkshire and two in Manchester. At first it was thought that he only targeted prostitutes, but after a time it became clear that this was not so. For example, Barbara Leach, who was murdered in September 1979 in Bradford, was a student at Bradford University.

The attacks created an atmosphere of intense anxiety in Bradford and the other towns and cities of West Yorkshire. This lasted for several years.

The police operation to apprehend the Ripper was one of the largest ever undertaken in the UK, at one stage involving 300 police officers. However, the investigation was seriously flawed. Sutcliffe himself was interviewed by the police on nine separate occasions, but the police became convinced that the murderer was from Sunderland, for they had been sent an audio tape on which the speaker had a Wearside accent. The tape eventually proved to be bogus. Sutcliffe was convicted and sentenced to life imprisonment in May 1981. (M. Bilton, *Wicked Beyond Belief*)

16 June

On this day the National Museum of Photography, Film and Television (renamed the National Media Museum in 2006) opened in Bradford. The museum is part of the Science Museum Group and its location in Bradford was part of a strategy aimed at ensuring that some national museums would be located in the regions, rather than in London. One feature of the museum was IMAX, the largest cinema screen in Britain at that time. The museum closed in 1997 for refurbishment and was reopened in 1999 by Pierce Brosnan, the fifth actor to portray James Bond on screen.

In 2009 the museum was instrumental – in partnership with other bodies – in launching Bradford's successful bid to become the world's first UNESCO City of Film. In 2011 the museum was voted the best indoor attraction in Yorkshire, and it has been one of the most visited museums in the North of England since it opened.

However, for a time in 2013 the museum was under threat of closure as part of the government's austerity measures. This led to a very strong campaign to keep the museum open, supported by such people as the eminent American film director Martin Scorsese, who had himself delivered a lecture at the museum in 1986. The campaign was successful and the National Media Museum remains open as one of Bradford's principal visitor attractions. (*Telegraph and Argus*, 2011)

11 May

On this day fifty-six people were killed and more than 250 injured when the main stand at Valley Parade football ground was destroyed by fire during a match between Bradford City and Lincoln City.

Shortly before half-time a small fire broke out in the stand, probably the result of a discarded cigarette or match. The stand was an old wooden affair, due to be replaced that summer, and the fire spread so rapidly that within four minutes the whole structure was ablaze. Although the police urged spectators to come on to the safety of the pitch, many sought to leave via the exits at the rear of the stand, but the doors there had been locked. This was the area where many died. Others, trapped in their seats, were burned to death by falling debris.

As is frequently the case, a terrible catastrophe can bring out the best in people. More than fifty people, police and members of the public, received bravery awards for rescuing people from the blaze that afternoon, often despite being badly burned themselves.

The official enquiry concluded that nobody was to blame for the tragedy. Over £4 million was raised in the following months for a disaster fund to which people from all over the world contributed. A memorial to those who died stands in Centenary Square outside City Hall. (P. Firth, *Four Minutes to Hell*)

14 December

On this day the Ray Honeyford saga finally came to an end and Honeyford accepted a reported £71,000 package in settlement of all existing claims against Bradford Council.

Ray Honeyford was appointed head teacher of Drummond Middle School in 1980. The school was in the heart of Manningham and most of its pupils were from Asian families. In 1984, Honeyford wrote an article entitled 'Education and Race – an Alternative View', which was published in *The Salisbury Review*, a right-wing journal. In his article Honeyford examined what he believed to be the factors that were hindering the educational performance of his Asian pupils. His argument was that immigrant families should be more in tune with the cultural norms of the indigenous host community. He also stated that the acquisition of a good standard of English should be a priority for Bradford's Asian populace.

This caused uproar in some quarters. The school was picketed by political activists, and Honeyford and his supporters were branded as racists. Meanwhile, Bradford Council dithered. Honeyford was first disciplined, later dismissed, then reinstated and finally persuaded to take early retirement with a pay-off.

Since that time many people have suggested that Honeyford may have had a point; multiculturalism – if taken to extremes – may lead to a form of segregation within which ethnic minorities can suffer a lack of proper opportunity. (J. Greenhalf, *It's a Mean Old Scene*)

19 September

Adrian Moorhouse won the gold medal in the men's 100-metres breaststroke swimming event at the Seoul Olympic Games on this date. He recorded a time of 1 minute 2.4 seconds. Born in Bradford and brought up in Bingley, Moorhouse was educated at Bradford Grammar School. His wool merchant father, Clifford, estimated that his unwavering support for his son's swimming career had cost him at least £10,000 per year, but clearly it was money well spent.

Moorhouse's ambition to strike Olympic gold started when he saw David Wilkie win a gold medal at the 1976 Montreal Olympics. From that time onward he undertook a relentless training regime which soon required him to swim every day for two hours before breakfast, followed by two and a half hours later in the afternoon or evening.

Between 1981 and 1987, Moorhouse was the British 100-metres breaststroke champion on six occasions and the 200-metres champion five times. In addition, during the same period, he won two Commonwealth Games gold medals and three European Championship gold medals.

Moorhouse gained further Commonwealth and European swimming honours after Seoul. He retired soon after the Barcelona Olympics in 1992, where he came eighth in the 100-metres final. He was awarded an MBE in 1989. After retiring he became a management consultant. (D. Lister, *Bradford's Own*)

14 January

This date saw a large group of men gather in the Tyrls, between the magistrates' court and City Hall, to protest about the publication of *The Satanic Verses*. This book, written by Salman Rushdie, had provoked outrage among Muslim communities in many countries, for it was seen as being grossly insulting to Islam.

It is possible that a conventional demonstration against *The Satanic Verses* would have passed off almost unnoticed in the city, but this one involved burning a copy of *The Satanic Verses,* and that made all the difference. Whilst a book-burning might be an accepted feature of protests in other parts of the world, in Europe it is always associated with the book-burnings carried out in Nazi Germany, an association made all the more painful in Bradford because many of its citizens are descendants of families which had been brutally treated by the Nazi regime.

Images of the Bradford book-burning went around the globe. Exactly one month after the event Ayatollah Khomeini issued his fatwa, stating that it was the sacred duty of all devout Muslims to kill Salman Rushdie, if they got the chance. Rushdie, fearing for his life, went into hiding for the next ten years. (J. Greenhalf, *It's a Mean Old Scene*)

27 March

Queen Elizabeth II and the Duke of Edinburgh visited Bradford to commemorate the centenary of Bradford being granted the status of a city. The day was also Maundy Thursday and the queen performed the traditional Maundy ceremony of distributing small bags of money to people selected for their contribution to the community. This took place at a service in Bradford Cathedral. Afterwards the royal party was driven to the newly designated Centenary Square, where the Bradford Youth Orchestra accompanied a choir of schoolchildren singing 'A Whole New World'. The queen laid a wreath on the Bradford City fire disaster memorial, which stands in Centenary Square.

After lunch with the lord mayor and lady mayoress (Councillor Gordon Mitchell and Mrs Mitchell) in City Hall, the queen and the duke were driven to Bradford City's Valley Parade football stadium. Here the queen formally opened the new stand on the Midland Road side of the stadium. This was not the stand in which fifty-six people had lost their lives in the terrible fire disaster twelve years earlier; that had already been replaced and the stadium as a whole had been extensively rebuilt. The brand new Midland Road stand was an important piece of this rebuilding programme. This was probably the only time in her long reign that the queen officially opened a football stand. (J. Appleby and J. Greenhalf, *Telegraph and Argus Stories of the Century*)

7 July

In the afternoon and evening of 7 July, a serious riot took place in the Whetley Hill area of the city. The British National Party (BNP) had planned a rally in Bradford and, convinced that the BNP and its supporters were out in force, a large group of Asian men gathered mid-afternoon to confront them.

Police in riot gear were quickly deployed. The police tactics were to drive the Asian group away from the city centre, back along Westgate and White Abbey Road. However, at Whetley Hill the angry crowd stood its ground and the police found it impossible to make progress. For several hours the police faced a crowd of several hundred men, who pelted them with bricks, stones, petrol bombs and fireworks.

More than 300 police officers were injured during the riot and fifty-five arrests were made at the time. Eventually a total of 297 arrests were made, 187 people were charged with riot – an unprecedented number in British legal history – and forty-five with violent disorder. A total of 200 jail sentences were handed down; many of those found guilty of riot received five years in prison.

The cost of the riot was £3.4 million for the police operation, plus a further £7.4 million of damage. However, the longer-term damage to Bradford's image was probably incalculable. (J. Bujra and J. Pearce, *Saturday Night and Sunday Morning: The 2001 Bradford Riot and Beyond*)

18 November

In the afternoon of this day, PC Sharon Beshenivsky was shot and killed when responding to reports of a robbery at a travel agent in Morley Street in the centre of Bradford. PC Beshenivsky was with her colleague, PC Teresa Millburn, when they confronted three men who had just robbed the agent of about £5,000. Both police constables were shot at point-blank range. Teresa Millburn survived the shooting, but Sharon Beshenivsky was fatally wounded.

Those responsible were apprehended and brought to trial, although it was 2007 before one of them, Mustaf Jama, was extradited from Somalia, where he had fled after the killing. He and two others were found guilty of murder and sentenced to life imprisonment with a thirty-five-year tariff. Three other men who had acted as lookouts and get-away drivers were convicted of manslaughter, robbery and firearms offences. They were also given lengthy prison sentences.

Sharon Beshenivsky was the seventh female police officer to have been killed on duty in Great Britain and the second to have been fatally shot; the first was PC Yvonne Fletcher who was shot in 1984 outside the Libyan Embassy.

In 2009, Prime Minister Gordon Brown unveiled a memorial at the location of Sharon Beshenivsky's murder, and a memorial bench stands in the reception area at Odsal Stadium, the home of Bradford Bulls. (*The Independent*, 2005)

24 May

On this day the queen and the Duke of Edinburgh attended the official opening of the Lakshmi Narayan Temple in Leeds Road. This temple (or mandir) is the largest Hindu place of worship in the North of England.

According to the 2001 census, Bradford had a total population of about 465,000, of whom 20 per cent were of Asian heritage and included Sikhs, Hindus and Muslims, with the last group being the largest. From the early 1960s onwards many Muslim families with origins in Kashmir, Pakistan and Bangladesh settled in Bradford, and over the years some inner-city suburbs, such as Manningham, Frizinghall and Girlington, have become predominantly Muslim Asian.

In 1985, Mohammed Ajeeb became Bradford's lord mayor – the first man of Pakistani heritage to attain this status in a major British city, and in 2011 Mrs Naveeda Ikram became Bradford's first female Muslim lord mayor.

Right from the start of its rapid industrialisation in the early part of the nineteenth century, Bradford has attracted immigrants from far and wide. By the twenty-first century, in addition to those from the Indian sub-continent, there were citizens who had their roots in central and Eastern Europe, in the former Yugoslavia, in sub-Saharan Africa, in the West Indies, and many other places. In 2010, because of its long history of welcoming people from all over the world, Bradford was deservedly given the status of City of Sanctuary. (A. Hall, *The Story of Bradford*)

2012

24 March

City Park was officially opened in the centre of Bradford on this date. This is a 6-acre public space right in the heart of the city and next to City Hall, which it complements very effectively. City Park contains the largest man-made water feature in any UK city, comprising a 4,000 square metre mirror pool with laser lighting and 100 fountains, the tallest of which can produce a jet 30 metres high, making it the highest fountain in Britain.

City Park was originally conceived in 2003 and, despite the failure to secure funding from the National Lottery, work commenced in 2009. Its construction was not without controversy, as some critics said that the cost of £24.4 million far outweighed any benefits that might be gained. Bradford Council, however, estimated that City Park could generate £80 million per annum for the city's economy. In order to achieve this, a series of events that made best use of the park was arranged. Of these the most impressive to date has been the BBC Television Bollywood-style spectacular production of *Carmen*, which was staged in City Park on 9 June 2013. This produced a very positive reaction throughout the country to City Park and to Bradford itself.

In 2013, City Park won an award from the Academy of Urbanism, which judged it to be the Best Place in the UK and Ireland. (*The Guardian*, 2012)

13 November

On this date the Lord Mayor of Bradford, Councillor Mike Gibbons, performed the traditional 'topping-out' ceremony of the Broadway Shopping Centre in the heart of Bradford.

The building of the shopping centre had a history mired in controversy. Demolition of existing buildings had commenced in 2004, and by 2006 the site had been cleared. But the scheduled opening date of 2007 came and went and nothing had been built; further developments were mothballed in 2010 because of the downturn in the UK economy. All that could be seen was a large open space surrounding what was soon disparagingly known as 'Bradford's hole in the ground'. Was the whole project a ghastly and expensive mistake, as the doom-mongers were saying?

But Bradford Council kept faith with the developers, Westfield, and the pessimists were eventually proved wrong. In early 2014, building work on the £270 million scheme finally commenced, and the centre was scheduled to open in time for Christmas 2015.

Together with the opening of City Park in 2012, the construction of the Broadway Shopping Centre was seen by the cautiously optimistic as something of a catalyst – a symbol of better times ahead. Other nothern cities, notably Leeds and Manchester, had started to thrive again. Was Bradford at last starting on the long road towards regaining some of its former weath, status and self-confidence? Perhaps things were looking up. (*Telegraph and Argus*, 2014)

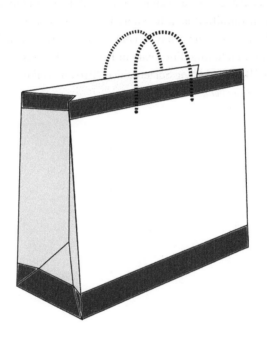

About the Author

ALAN HALL gained a degree in English at Durham University and then qualified as a teacher. For the next thirty-seven years he taught in a variety of comprehensive schools in West Yorkshire, including nine years in Bradford. He has been the Chair of Bradford Civic Society since 2010 and is the author of *The Story of Bradford*.

Bibliography and Further Reading

Appleby, Jim and Jim Greenhalf, *Telegraph and Argus Stories of the Century*
    (Breedon Books, 1999)
Aronsfeld, C.C., *German Jews in 19th Century Bradford*, Vol. 53 (Yorkshire
    Archaeological Journal, 1981)
Bilton, Michael, *Wicked Beyond Belief* (Harper Perennial, 2006)
Bonnington, Chris, *Annapurna South Face* (Book Faith, 1971)
Bradford Art Galleries and Museums (ed.), *The Face of Worstedopolis* (Bradford
    Art Galleries and Museums, 1982)
Bradford Library Service (ed.), *The Siege of Bradford* (Bradford Library Service,
    date unknown)
Bujra, Janet and Jenny Pearce, *Saturday Night and Sunday Morning: The 2001
    Bradford Riot and Beyond* (Vertical Editions, 2011)
Burne and Young, *The Battle of Adwalton Moor* (unpublished essay, Bradford
    Library Service, 1959)
Clark, Colin and Reuben Davison, *In Loving Memory: The Story of Undercliffe
    Cemetery* (Sutton Publishing, 2004)
Coates, D.M., *Bradford City Tramways* (Wyvern Publications, 1984)
Cudworth, William, *Historical Notes on the Bradford Corporation* (Thomas Brear, 1881)
Cudworth, William, *Life and Correspondence of Abraham Sharp* (Sampson Low, 1889)
Cudworth, William, *Round About Bradford* (first edn 1874, republished by
    Mountain Press, 1968)
Cudworth, William, *Worstedopolis: A Sketch History of the Town and Trade of Bradford*
    (first edn 1888, republished by The Old Bradfordian Press, 1997)
Duckett, B. (ed.), *Bradford Chapters* (Propagator Press, 2007)
Duckett, B. (ed.), *The German Immigrants: Their Influence in 19th Century Bradford*
    (Propagator Press, 2007)
Duckett, B. and J. Waddington-Feather, *Bradford, History & Guide* (Tempus, 2005)
Ellison, D.B., *Bradford on the Eve of the Civil War* (unpublished essay, Bradford
    Library Service)
Fieldhouse, Joseph, *Bradford* (Longman, 1972)
Firth, Gary, *A History of Bradford* (Phillimore, 1997)
Firth, Gary, *J.B. Priestley's Bradford* (Tempus, 2006)
Firth, Paul, *Four Minutes to Hell* (Parrs Wood Press, 2005)
Greenhalf, Jim, *It's a Mean Old Scene: A History of Modern Bradford from 1974*
    (Redbeck Press, 2003)

Griffith, Frances Mary and Christine Lynch, *Reflections on the Cottingley Fairies* (JMJ Publications, 2009)

Hall, Alan, *The Story of Bradford* (The History Press, 2013)

Hird, Horace, *Bradford Remembrancer* (McDonald Book Co. Ltd, 1972)

Holdsworth, Peter, *The Rebel Tyke; Bradford and J.B. Priestley* (Bradford Libraries, 1994)

Hugman, Barry, *Football League Players Records* (Williams Publications, 1981)

James, David, *Bradford* (Ryburn Publishing, 1990)

James, John, *History of Bradford* (Longmans, 1866; republished by Morten, 1973)

James, John, *History of the Worsted Manufacture in England* (first edn 1857, republished by Cass & Co., 1968)

James, John, *History and Topography of Bradford* (Longmans, 1841)

King, Stanley, *Bradford Corporation Trolleybuses* (Venture Publications, 1994)

Leach, Peter and Nikolaus, *The Buildings of England: Yorkshire West Riding: Leeds, Bradford and the North* (Yale UP, 2009)

Lister, Derek, *Bradford's Own* (Sutton Publishing, 2004)

McMillan, Margaret, *The Life of Rachel McMillan* (Dent, 1927)

Parker, B.J.R. (ed.), *Education in Bradford 1870–1970* (Educational Services Committee, Bradford Corporation, 1970)

Pearce, Cyril, *The Manningham Mills Strike* (University of Hull, 1975)

Povey, Ralph, *The History of the Keighley and Worth Valley Railway* (Keighley and Worth Valley Preservation Society, 1970)

Pratt, Michael, *The Influence of the Germans on Bradford* (unpublished essay, Margaret McMillan College, Bradford, 1971)

Priestley, J.B., *English Journey* (Heinemann, 1934)

Raw, David, *Bradford Pals* (Pen and Sword, 2006)

Reynolds, Jack, *Saltaire* (Bradford Art Galleries and Museums, 1976)

Richardson, C., *The Bradford Region* (Bradford Libraries, Archives and Information Service, 2002)

Sheeran, George, *The Buildings of Bradford* (Tempus, 2005)

Sheeran, George, *The Bradford Poisoning of 1858* (Ryburn Publishing, 1992)

Suddards, Roger, (ed.) *Titus of Salt* (Watmough, 1976)

Taylor, Simon and Kathryn Gibson, *Manningham: Character and Diversity in a Bradford Suburb* (English Heritage, 2010)

Whitaker, A. and B. Myland, *Railway Memories No. 4: Bradford* (Bellcode Books, 1993)

Wolfe, Humbert, *Now A Stranger* (Cassell, 1933)

Woods, Mike and T. Platts (eds), *Bradford in the Great War* (Sutton, 2007)

Wright, D.G., *The Chartist Risings in Bradford* (Bradford Libraries, 1987)

www.leedsbradfordairport.co.uk (official website, accessed 2014)

Newspaper Articles

Telegraph and Argus, 29 November 2007; 2 December 2010; 21 September 2011; 13 November 2014

The Independent, 20 November 2005

The Guardian, 19 February 2012

Also from The History Press

GREAT WAR BRITAIN

Great War Britain is a unique new local series to mark the centenary of the Great War. In partnership with archives and museums across Great Britain, the series provides an evocative portrayal of life during this 'war to end all wars'. In a scrapbook style, and beautifully illustrated, it includes features such as personal memoirs, letters home, diary extracts, newspaper reports, photographs, postcards and other local First World War ephemera.

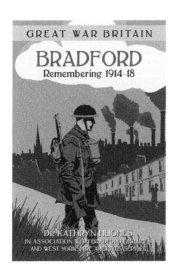

Find these titles and more at
www.thehistorypress.co.uk

Lightning Source UK Ltd.
Milton Keynes UK
UKOW07f1142040215

245676UK00002B/2/P